Gender and organizational change

# Gender and organizational change

## Bridging the gap between policy and practice

*Mandy Macdonald*
*Ellen Sprenger*
*Ireen Dubel*

Royal Tropical Institute – The Netherlands

Royal Tropical Institute
KIT Press
Mauritskade 63
P.O. Box 95001
1090 HA Amsterdam
The Netherlands
Telephone: +31 (20) 5688272
Telefax: +31 (20) 5688286
E-mail: kitpress@kit.nl

The publisher gratefully acknowledges the contribution of Novib and Hivos to the realization of this book, which originated in a Gender Working Group workshop (June 1995), hosted by these organizations.

Cover illustration: Marion Jurriaans
Cover design: Ad van Helmond
Printing: Krips - Meppel
ISBN: 90 6832 709 7
NUGI: 661

Printed and bound in the Netherlands

# Table of contents

adapted to new ways of understanding gender relations. They have recognized that power inequalities within the family and other aspects of people's lives previously considered 'private', such as violence against women and women's reproductive health and rights, are important social and developmental issues. As a result of this analysis, donor NGOs (referred to in this book as NGDOs) now support many women's initiatives in the South which are concerned not only with meeting women's specific needs, in a compensatory way, within an overall context of gender inequality, but which also – and more importantly – defend and advance women's human rights and strive for equal rights and opportunities for women and men.

At previous *Eurostep* gender workshops, attention was given principally to aspects of the promotion of gender equality in counterpart organizations.[3] The workshops identified the need for European NGDOs to analyse gender inequality in their own internal structures, systems, and cultures as well as in their work with counterpart organizations, but did not deal with the theme in any detail. In 1995 the Gender Working Group (GWG) decided to turn the spotlight on European donor agencies themselves and to focus explicitly on the theme of internal gender equality, as a logical sequel to the attention given in earlier workshops to mainstreaming,[4] gender in the partnership relationship, and lobbying and advocacy work on gender. Without attention to gender sensitivity and a commitment to gender equality inside donor organizations, the gap between policy and practice can never be fully bridged.

This workshop started, then, from the premise that, although much has happened to address the question of gender equality in development, we have been unable to affect the gendered core, and therefore the product, of organizations – including donor organizations. If we were to compare an organization to a living organism, say a human being, we should be aiming to change the heart itself, not just a leg or an arm, or the appendix. Making changes in the heart of an organization is an important prerequisite for changing its gendered outcomes, and is key to understanding and bridging this policy - practice gap.

With this book we hope to contribute to the ongoing debate on this topic. We aim to take a practical approach to gender in relation to issues of organizational change, and hope to provide readers with some concrete tools that will support them in their quest to make a difference in the gendered outcomes of their agencies, and ultimately in the lives of women and men among the resource-poor and marginalized.

## Gender and organizational change

There is today a rich and extensive body of documentation and literature dealing with women's subordinate position vis-à-vis men and the gendered nature and outcomes of development processes. The UNDP's *Human development report* (UNDP, 1995), for example, states that there is as yet no country where women and men enjoy equal rights and opportunities. Increasing numbers of so-called mainstream organizations have responded by formulating elaborate and detailed policy statements. Feminist discourse and insights have been incorporated into the policies of development bureaucracies such as the World Bank, United Nations agencies, national governments' overseas development ministries, international and national NG(D)Os and funding agencies. There is no doubt that gender is on the international agenda. But to what extent have these institutions *themselves* really changed their practice? Are they accountable to the needs and aspirations of women? What role is there for the women who have entered these agencies with the objective of 'breaking in and speaking out?'[5] Can historically male-dominated development agencies be transformed to an extent that goes beyond supporting the occasional women's project or appointing a gender expert?

Growing awareness and understanding of the developmental relevance of the gender hierarchy has had an undeniable effect on the policy and practice of Northern donor NGDOs. They have asked questions such as:

- what interventions are strategic and appropriate in order to set in motion a process of organizational change and learning as regards gender equality?
- what can Northern NG(D)Os contribute in their role as external funding agencies?

Many of them, after a process of institutional learning, have developed policies recognizing the legitimacy of women's struggles for empowerment in the South and seeking to support them. Hivos and Novib, for instance, have developed targets for support to women's organizations that address gender issues through advocacy work and development of alternative interventions aiming at strengthening civil society at large.[6]

Besides setting targets, donor agencies have developed procedures to ensure that each and every organization which qualifies for their support is assessed and regularly monitored in terms of its gendered outcomes. They have given much attention to formulating and incorporating performance thresholds and other conditions pertaining to gender equality in their work with counterpart organizations. Most agencies have relevant instruments in place which include gender criteria: for example, assessment procedures for funding, reporting requirements, monitoring guidelines, terms of reference for evaluations, and country policy documents.

But an important result of that new, strategic support for women's organizations in the South is that it has led to a new relationship, or accountability mechanism, in which Southern women's organizations have been able to draw the attention of Northern NGDOs to the persistent gender inequalities in donor practice. Recent evaluations, for instance that carried out by Hivos during 1993–1995, of the impact of a donor's gender policy and interventions on its mixed counterpart organizations in the South, revealed the magnitude of the challenge of overcoming resistance to addressing gender inequalities in counterpart organizations. But it also became clear that one source of that resistance is the perception counterparts have of persistent gender inequalities in the donor organization itself. Reasonably, counterparts ask whether they should be expected to expend resources and energy on striving for greater gender equality while donor agencies do not address those issues in a consistent manner in their own organizations.

## GENDER: SOME DEFINITIONS

### What is gender?

The primary dictionary meaning of the word 'gender' is 'the grammatical classification of nouns and related words, roughly corresponding to the two sexes and sexlessness' (*Concise Oxford Dictionary of Current English*, 8th edn, 1990). In the social sciences, the term 'gender' has been introduced to refer to differences between women and men without strictly biological connotations, *socially constructed* differences to the two sexes although they are not caused by biological sexual differences. Gender relations are the rules, traditions, and social relationships in societies and cultures which together determine what is considered 'feminine' and what 'masculine', and how power is allocated between, and used differently by, women and men. Gender refers to a social construction of femininity and masculinity which varies over time and place and is enacted through learned, rather than innate, behaviour.

Thus, the struggle for women's equality with men – and its naming as the struggle for gender equality – is based on the recognition that gender inequality is caused by structural and institutional discrimination. Gender awareness involves understanding the difference between sex roles and gender roles, and understanding that the latter, being socially and historically determined and constructed, can be changed. A gender perspective and gender awareness are based on the principle of gender equality as an objective.

### Development, women, and gender

The great value of gender as an analytical concept is that it directs attention towards social and cultural processes and interventions in terms of their differential effects on women, men, and the relationships between women and men. It does not look at women in isolation and it enables differences between women and men, and between different groups of women, due, for example, to class, race, ethnicity, age, ability, and sexuality to become visible.

Acknowledgement of the unequal relations between the sexes in development is of course not new. But until relatively recently Northern policy-makers and practitioners working in this area concentrated primarily on women in the development process: first highlighting the disadvantages they suffer and later recognizing their positive contribution to development, but usually seeing attention to women's needs as something *additional* to the main thrust of development' (the 'women in development' – WID – approach). The organizational expression of the WID approach has been the establishment, in governments and NG(D)Os, of separate (often underresourced and peripheral) structures bearing the mandate for women, with the result that 'mainstream' structures have not incorporated women's issues and interests. Interventions have typically taken the form of women-specific policies, programmes and projects, while the problem of unequal gender relations in political spaces occupied by both women and men has remained unaddressed.

Since the mid–1980s, however, there has been a growing recognition that an analysis of gender relations which deals only with women is incomplete; and the focus has shifted towards the unequal division of labour, power, and resources between *women and men* in societies and the different ways women and men are affected by policies and programmes which claim to offer equal benefits to everyone in a community. The focus is on gender relations as a necessary category in the analysis of social relations (the 'gender and development' – GAD – approach). The organizational expression of this approach is a combination of separate structures and the promotion of gender expertise within existing (mixed) structures. The mandate of GAD structures goes beyond women to examine the balance of power between women and men. Women-specific interventions and interventions aimed at integration are not seen as mutually exclusive strategies, but as strategic choices to be employed as appropriate.

While the WID approach was valid and necessary to make women *visible* in the development process, and while there are still strong arguments giving priority to women's development and encouraging the growth of women's organizations, the main weakness of the WID approach is that is has tended to generate ad-hoc or 'add-on' solutions, at worst resulting in tokenism and marginalization of women's long-term interests.

The GAD approach has had its problems, too. Since gender refers to both women and men, it has been easy to misconstrue gender as a neutral concept, obscuring or denying the fact that, in the world as it is at present, gender relations are a hierarchy with men at the top. A gender analysis, therefore, is not just a question of identifying differences, but of analysing how these differences have led to inequalities in power between women and men. Nonetheless, by bringing the *interdependence* of women and men in society into the foreground, the GAD approach leads to the crucial recognition that *no problem or issue is gender-neutral*.

In short, a gender approach implies the adoption of strategies to redress gender-based inequalities and hierarchies of power. Such strategies may focus on women or men separately, or on women and men together. However, since gender relations almost universally favour men and disadvantage women, explicit and ongoing recognition of women's subordinate position in the gender hierarchy is necessary.

**The gender portmanteau**

Today, 'gender' is part of the everyday vocabulary of most development policy-makers and practitioners: so much so, in fact, that the term has become something of a portmanteau word, often being used rather loosely to encompass any of a range of concepts to do with the development of a gender analysis or perspective and the policy choices and implementation strategies consequent upon such an analysis. Thus, *gender issues* are issues concerning gender relations; a *gender policy* is a policy which addresses the problem of unequal gender relations in a given context; a *gender focal point/person* is (ideally) a staff member or administrative unit with responsibility for overseeing the formulation and implementation of policies on gender relations; and so on. This use of 'gender' can have the unfortunate effect of obscuring the finer meaning intended: 'integrating gender', for instance, tends to be used to mean either making a gender analysis of a given issue or incorporating elements aiming at greater gender equality into a policy, programme or project.

'Gender' has also become a 'politically correct' term, and thus tends to be overused and used loosely, often conveying the right political message at the expense of accurate meaning. Most notably in this context, 'gender' is now often used when 'women' is what is really meant (which means that a project which really targets only women can be disguised as a more politically acceptable project aiming to redress gender-based imbalances). While we may occasionally be guilty in this book of using 'gender' as a shorthand for gender relations or a gender perspective, we have been rigorous in ensuring that when we refer to gender, we always mean the relations between women and men.

**The 'added value' of gender**

It is often asked what is the *added value* of incorporating gender considerations into the analysis of development issues and the strategies for confronting development problems. The question is misleading. The gender dimension cannot be 'added' to an agency's values or practice; it is already there, because all aspects of the agency's functioning are affected by gender relations within the agency and in its relations with its interlocutors. The point is rather that without an analysis of gender relations and attention to making them more equal, you get bad development. Development without a gender perspective is only half of development: if one gender is left behind, there cannot be real development even for the dominant gender. Working towards a gender-aware organization thus means *changing the gender-based power balance in the direction of greater equality.*

---

So – much more recently – Northern donor agencies have begun to look at their own internal policies and practices as regards gender relations. This means asking questions such as:
- do we practise at home what we preach abroad?
- if not, how do those double standards affect the quality of our interventions and our credibility in the eyes of counterpart organizations?
- how can an organization be restructured and its priorities reoriented so as to make it more gender-equal (for instance via an affirmative action programme) with limited – or even dwindling – resources?

- as organizations working on overseas development, what do we gain (and what can we contribute?) by forming alliances with women's organizations in our own countries?

The *Eurostep* workshop invited participants to look at issues close to home in our own countries, rather than 'out there' in the South; to break through the façades of our institutions and examine how the structures, systems, culture, and relations of power in our own organizations are gendered and therefore produce gendered outcomes. If we take as a point of departure the view that a gender analysis and strategy should be an integral part of any work undertaken by an organization, what fundamental adjustments and processes of organizational change would be required to make this a practical reality? What would be useful entry points for promoting organizational change from a gender perspective? How should men be included in debates on gender and changes in practice?

The workshop also looked at the role of the change agents whose aim is to promote such processes of change, and tried to identify tools and strategies that could be helpful at different stages. As gender experts or staff responsible for gender issues in Northern donor agencies, we are forced to acknowledge that very few of us have experience or training in management and organizational development in the general sense. While managers in donor NGDOs – frequently as a result of pressure from gender experts and/or women staff of their organizations – are increasingly becoming sensitized to gender issues, and most have had some exposure to gender training, gender experts are less likely to have done management training courses or to have learned skills in management-related areas such as negotiation, conflict resolution, problem-solving, or leadership. For this reason, the contributions to the workshop of the Dutch consultancy group De Beuk, which works on issues of management and diversity in organizations, added a new dimension to the discussion.


## Focus and readership

Organizations and other collective endeavours are our point of entry into gender debates and the subject of our interventions as development agencies. As Northern-based donor organizations, we work with other organizations. Our work is founded on the principle that people can achieve change in society more effectively if they are organized than they can if they are acting as individuals. Thus, we envisage that this book will be of practical interest primarily to people who work in, or are members of, organizations.

Initially we intended only to produce a simple report of the *Eurostep* workshop for participants and *Eurostep* member agencies. However, during the process of compiling the report we began to feel that our deliberations could be of interest to a wider audience of gender and development practitioners working with and within development agencies, in both the North and the South. Women from the South who attended the workshop had been keen to hear how Northern donor NGDOs had begun to integrate

Finally, we are grateful to Novib and Hivos for funding both the workshop and the preparation of the book.

## Notes

1. Such as the UN Conference on Environment and Development (UNCED), Rio de Janeiro, 1992; the UN Conference on Human Rights, Vienna, 1993; the International Conference on Population and Development (ICPD), Cairo, 1994; and the World Summit on Social Development (WSSD), Copenhagen, March 1995.

2. *Eurostep* stands for European Solidarity Towards Equal Participation of People. The network was formed in 1990 as an advocacy-oriented network of European secular NGDOs and has a secretariat in Brussels. It contains 21 member organizations from 15 European countries. These organizations work on development and rehabilitation in 90 countries in Africa, Asia, Latin America, the Middle East, and Eastern Europe, working with over 3,000 NGO counterparts around the world. See Appendix for list of member organizations.

In 1993 *Eurostep* set up a special network on gender issues, called the Gender Working Group (GWG). The GWG has a gender advocacy agenda, works towards mainstreaming gender in *Eurostep*'s advocacy work, and acts as a pressure group within the member agencies to promote change which will ensure the development and implementation of gender policies. Members of the GWG are staff members of the member agencies with specific responsibility for gender issues (gender focal people) and other staff committed to working for gender equality in the organization and its counterparts. The GWG meets at least once a year at a workshop devoted to a current theme, such as planning from a gender perspective (1993), gender and partnership (1994), gender and organizational change (1995), or ensuring a gender perspective in all *Eurostep*'s advocacy work and documents (1996). Increasingly, representatives of counterpart organizations accompany *Eurostep* members at the annual meeting. The Gender Task Force is a smaller group of active GWG members plus the *Eurostep* secretariat. It meets regularly to develop and implement *Eurostep*'s advocacy programme on gender equality.

3. The relationship between Northern NGDOs and Southern NGOs is a complex one due to the power inequality related to the donor-recipient equation. The concept of counterpart organizations relates to the notion of a partnership in development. Northern NGDOs and Southern NGOs ideally position themselves as partners in a shared cause: the eradication of poverty, counteracting processes of marginalization and strengthening of civil society based on values of human rights, justice and participatory democracy for all.

4. 'Mainstreaming' is the term used to describe strategies aimed at integrating a gender perspective into all aspects of an organization, i.e. its mission, strategies, programmes, structure, systems and culture, rather than maintaining a separate women's programme.

5. This was the title of a workshop organized at the NGO Forum in Beijing by the Institute of Development Studies, Sussex University, Great Britain.

6. Cebemo, Hivos, Icco and Novib, 'With quality in mind: final report on the measures taken by Cebemo, Hivos, Icco and Novib in response to the impact study. Produced by GOM, Oegstgeest, the Netherlands, March 1995.

7. The contributions of the external facilitators of the workshop – Febe Deug, Wanjiru Kihoro, and Aruna Rao – and their respective organizations are central: see in particular chapters 6 and 7.

Of the mass of theoretical work on these issues, emerging not only from development studies and gender studies, but also from the study of public administration and business structures, we are particularly indebted to the work of Anne-Marie Goetz on gender in institutions. Theoretical works cited in the course of the book appear in the bibliography.

- systems: the conditions and agreements relating to the manner in which processes (information, communication and decision-making) and flows (cash and goods) proceed;
- culture: the combined sum of the individual opinions, shared values and norms of the members of the organization.

These components may be more or less formally discussed and established, but can be identified in one form or another in most organizations, large or small, across the world. While distinct, these components are also closely interrelated: a change in any one of them will almost certainly imply change in some or all of the others.

While this is just one of a variety of ways of defining an organization,[1] and while it is open to debate (one might want, for instance, to separate the goals or vision of the organization from the strategies by which it works towards its goals, or to define organizational culture both more broadly and more subtly, as we shall see below in chapter 7), it gives a useful indication of the different levels at which change is to be sought. If gender sensitivity and ultimately gender equality are to take root at the very heart of an organization, they must be firmly incorporated into all of these aspects. Most theorists agree, however, that the most fundamental level at which transformation needs to take place is that of organizational culture, not only because it is informal, unwritten, and not often scrutinized or evaluated in the same way as the organization's financial health, the efficiency of its structures and procedures, or the success of its external interventions, but also because organizational culture touches on the beliefs and value systems of individuals and is thus the point at which the personal really does become political in the organization. No matter how radically structures and systems may be reformed, if organizational culture is unchanged the changes will remain superficial, cosmetic, and ultimately without effect.

Other factors also influence the characteristics of organizations: their origins and history, and the external environment in which they operate. An analysis of an organization which includes these factors might take account of the following oppositions:

- past and future: what is the organization's history, and what are its visions and perspectives for the future?
- inside and outside: what is the relationship between the organization's internal structures, systems, and culture and the external environment in which it works and which impacts upon it?
- top and bottom: within the organization, what are the dynamics between the top levels (senior management) and the base? In the partnership relation, what is the donor/counterpart dynamic?

**Organizational change and the learning organization**

Organizational change depends on collective learning by the organization. This means that the organization has to be open to learning and prepared to develop mechanisms for organizational learning; there needs to be a willingness for change felt in common by a critical mass of staff or members of the organization, so that the goal of change becomes an institutional goal rather than merely the sum of the individual goals of people working within the organization. Where organizational changes in gender relations are at stake, this progression from individual to institutional willingness to change is particularly important. The fact that gender sensitivity and the capacity to deal with gender issues still tend to be too closely associated with particular individuals or personalities shows that many organizations have as yet not been able to institutionalize organizational learning or to develop an organizational memory.

First of all, the organization has to be *willing* to change, and above all to be able to perceive the need for change. The ability to perceive this need depends on the existence in the organization of a tradition of transparency and accountability – both internally, among staff members and between staff and management, and externally, towards counterparts and other interlocutors. If there is such a tradition and practice, the need to change will become apparent. Internal transparency in manager-staff relations can reveal problems in ways that persuade management of the need to change; while external accountability on the part of Southern counterparts to Northern donor agencies – and, as we have noted already, vice versa – can provide the catalyst for initiating processes of change towards more equal gender relations in the organization.

A learning organization is committed to the process of collective learning. It is open to change and able to be innovative. It not only gives its members or staff opportunities to learn as individuals (which is of limited value since there is no guarantee they will feed their learnings back into the organization); it builds *collective* knowledge and develops channels and forms of communication for systematizing such knowledge. It actively pursues a policy of increasing its organizational learning capacity continuously, by means of training, information systems, consultation processes at all levels of the organization (spanning different levels and sectors). Both managers and staff are aware of the importance of effective communication in the organization, and managers ensure that processes of organizational learning are adequately resourced and planned into the organization's activities. For instance, in an NGDO, processes of evaluation and analysis are used to gather and compare information and experience on good and bad practice, to draw the appropriate lessons from experience, and to internalize those lessons. The learning process is a process of collective learning, without teachers, in which everyone has to take part; it is also an unlearning process. Thus it is an experiential learning process, a combination of learning the new and unlearning the old (De Beuk, 1995: no. 9; Swieringa & Wierdsma, 1992: 66).

As we have noted above, transparency and accountability are key concepts in creating a learning organization. If there are strong, excluding barriers between managers and staff, organizational learning will be impeded and ultimately impossible, since the institutionalization of the learning depends crucially on its being taken on board by management.

As well as the division between management and base, there are two other divisions which can hinder open communication and therefore effective organizational learning:

# THREE LEVELS OF INSTITUTIONAL LEARNING

*Single-loop* learning is aimed at changing the *rules* which apply in an organization. Characteristic of single-loop learning is that the underlying theories, principles or assumptions themselves are not under discussion. Solutions are at the level of *improvement* – the same, but better. In particular, 'how?' questions rather than 'why?' questions are raised. Learning takes place at the level of arriving at agreements on what people are allowed or obliged to do, affecting behaviour with regard to rules.

*Double-loop* learning is about changing not only rules but also the underlying *insights*. Thus it concerns learning at the level of insight, involving 'why?' questions, questions at the level of collective knowledge and understanding. Double-loop learning typically addresses problems of conflicts and controversies between departments and/or individuals. That is, signals of the need for double-loop learning are:
- external signals, such as continuing complaints, which make it clear that adjustment of the rules does not help;
- internal signals, such as friction and lack of collective clarity, signals that the mutual relationship of rules is no longer understood.

The major reason problems are not solved by double-loop learning is avoidance of discussion of their background. This is a kind of flight: sometimes a flight into doing nothing at all; sometimes a flight into action (such as 'reorganization' – a bogus solution everyone knows won't work). A third solution, often the one chosen, is conflict.

On the other hand, double-loop learning can be *innovative*: it involves arriving at new insights, or the renewal of insights, within the framework of existing principles.

*Triple-loop* learning is involved if the essential *principles* on which the organization is based come under discussion. This level of learning is potentially transformative. It involves asking questions about what kind of organization we are and want to be, what values we consider important: what position we want to adopt in the outside world, our purpose and identity. This level of learning involves 'what for?' questions, questions about developing new principles with which the organization can move on to a new phase in its development. The change resulting from triple-loop learning is *development*.

A changing organization must take on learning at all three of these levels.[2]

that between thinkers and doers in the organization, and that between the organization and the external world (De Beuk, 1995: no. 9). In the latter case, it is necessary to have a critical understanding of how organizations themselves, however progressive, mirror dominant ideologies in the external world, particularly as regards gender roles and relations, and how, therefore, organizational learning may well take place within an ideology which itself needs to be challenged. 'When we look at learning and the production of knowledge in organizations we should ask where the learning is coming from .... Does learning replicate gendered structures?'[3]

The learning organization creates opportunities for collective learning which challenge and transcend these barriers, using loose networks throughout the organization or other decentralized fora. Organizational learning also implies unlearning, since changing attitudes and engrained patterns of behaviour involves learning to abandon behaviour and ways of working that have become routine and habitual, and questioning the rationale that led in the past to the establishment of those patterns.

This kind of learning is essential for collaborative organizational change. Effective and lasting change in an organization cannot be brought about by coercion, but by collective learning that works towards building consensus on the need for change and the kind of change needed. This learning process accepts that there will inevitably be psychological resistance to changes in fundamental attitudes. Resistance is natural and to be expected. It can arise from ignorance, fear, anxiety about a whole range of things. In a learning organization, this is acceptable; the response is dialogue and negotiation rather than confrontation.

For organizational change to be organic and democratic, it should have the following features.[4]

- The members of the organization must share a definition of the problem, and must 'own' the goals of change; they must have identified these, and the need for change, themselves. The goals cannot be imposed by the change agent.

- The role of the change agent is to help the organization reach the goals it has chosen. S/he is not an expert or a 'doctor', who diagnoses problems and prescribes 'cures', but a facilitator or catalyst, helping the organization to makes its own analysis and diagnosis and look for its own solutions. Of course, s/he may do this by offering tools for analysis, advice on methodologies and strategies, help in conflict resolution, etc.

- Just as long-term change is hoped for, so is the process long-term. This is not a quick fix, neither is it something that requires a one-off intervention after which the goal can be assumed to have been reached. It is a combination of education and lobbying, both of which build change by means of many small steps.

- The change must be both systemic and personal. It involves changes in culture, structure, procedures at the level of the organization as a whole, and learning and attitude change by individual members of the organization.

- The change must be tailored to the specific situation and needs of each organization rather than trying to make the organization conform to any externally-determined general model. It meets the specific requirements of the organization as identified by a collaborative process of data collection and analysis.

Finally – assuming that a climate for change exists – the change process, to be effective, must begin with analysis. The problem has to be identified before it can be solved. In the learning organization, analysis is also a collective process in which, perhaps with the help of a facilitator, the relevant data are gathered (via interviews, focus group discussions, review of policy documents and other documentation, etc.). The external context of the organization and the national and even wider trends within which it is functioning also need to be analysed; this process will be discussed in more detail in chapter 6.

Obviously, this is crucial in the case of gender. An analysis needs to be made of why gender relations are unequal and to what degree, within the organizational context and in the society in which the organization is operating. What gender relationships inflect the organization's values, objectives, and policy? How are they embodied in its practice? This is the subject of the next section.

## Organizations and diversity

Diversity is a concept often used in discussions about the ability to deal with differences within an organization. We take as a starting point the view that a good organization is an organization not only where different groups – men and women, people of different economic statuses, nationalities and ethnicities, people of different ages and abilities, and of different sexualities – are reasonably well represented numerically, but where the capacities, skills and contributions of these different people are being used to the optimum and as such improve the quality of the organization. In a situation where people of many ethnic backgrounds or languages work together, it is clearly essential to recognize and build on the positive aspects of diversity. This is equally true of gender relations: the concept of diversity stresses that variety in terms of positions of power, opportunities, capacities, and skills is organized along gender lines as well as on the basis of ethnicity, economic status, age, religion, sexuality, and so on.

### What makes an organization diverse?
The De Beuk consultancy in the Netherlands, which does extensive work on diversity in organizational development, has listed the characteristics by which a multicultural organization can be recognized (De Beuk, 1995: no. 27). These criteria can be applied

with very little modification to any organization which claims to be diverse in terms of ethnicity, class, gender, age, ability, sexuality, and so on. Diversity must be apparent in:

- the ethnic, gender, etc. composition of the management structures and the workforce, at all levels;
- the ways in which target groups feel addressed (policy, content and presentation; language and images);
- an internal policy with specific target-directed projects (if necessary) and attention to diversity within the regular internal policy;
- the naturalness of arrangements whereby black/immigrant, female, or other non-dominant-group employees do not work exclusively with their own target group or in target-directed projects;
- the possibility for employees who want to organize on the basis of one aspect of their identity (gender, sexuality, ethnicity, age, etc.) to do so, and for this activity to be given scope to enrich the whole institution's thinking and practice;
- an organizational culture in which:
  - etiquette, rules and rituals originate from different cultural backgrounds;
  - there is respect for differences and understanding for agreements linked to preparedness to allow for mutual influencing;
  - all differences which are loaded with power can be discussed;
  - tokenism and exclusion mechanisms for managing staff and colleagues as a group are recognized and addressed (the greater the diversity, the harder for tokenism to operate, since the 'dominant' group loses some of its dominance if many other groups are represented, even if each is in a minority);
  - gender, cultural/ethnic background, class, age, sexuality, professional identity are considered as coexistent and equally important aspects of people's identities and none is overemphasized or held to represent the whole person;
  - humour can be expressed, with certainty on all sides that the relationship between the majority and minority groups is good.

*What is necessary to ensure or safeguard diversity in an organization?*
De Beuk identifies the following requisites:

- a view of what multi-cultural (and gender-sensitive) cooperation is;
- an effort on all sides (white and black/immigrant, men and women, and so forth) to allow the cooperation to succeed in practice. Alertness to opportunities to use the handling of differences as mutual enrichment;
- a code of practice (not necessarily a formal one) for handling 'overstepping the mark' situations – situations of conscious or unconscious racism, sexism, or exclusion on other grounds;
- clarifying everyone's motives or self-interest in diversity. It is precisely when people formulate for themselves their own, specific interest in diversity that they are less likely to see diversity as a sort of charity towards 'others'.

An organization which is really committed to diversity – and also an organization which is really committed to gender equality – will pay attention to all these areas.

Fundamentally, respecting diversity is about redistribution of power, and a diverse organization that understands how to make use of its potential is one which gives space, respect, and a voice to people of all kinds.

Similarly, diversity among organizations grouped in networks and associations allows for the equal participation of organizations of differing sizes, perspectives, cultures, stages of development and degrees of wealth, within the basic parameters of common interest and values that brought the organizations together in the first place.

## Organizations and gender

Development is not gender-neutral: until very recently it has been development for men. Organizations, in both the South and the North, are not gender-neutral either, but are gendered in the same way society is gendered: men are dominant. There is, for instance, a sexual division of labour in organizations which mirrors that in society at large: men tend to predominate in the decision-making, public areas of an organization (e.g. as managers), women in the 'private', internal areas (as assistants, secretaries, librarians, catering and cleaning staff). Indeed Goetz (1995:3) would go further, asserting that

> gendered internal structures and practices actually produce gendered outcomes and personnel who, whatever their sex, reproduce gender-discriminatory outcomes.

That is, the structures themselves are patriarchal and meet men's needs better than those of women. Women may have a different approach to power and organizations than men; but women in mixed organizations have to operate within structures and systems basically designed for and by men and geared to their needs, and even women's organizations still have to operate within existing patriarchal institutional and macro-political contexts. An organization may become gender-aware and yet have difficulties achieving gender equality because it is still structured as before. Changes in structure and culture must thus go hand in hand. Feminist writers (e.g. Goetz, 1992, 1995; Longwe, 1995) confirm our own daily experience of this as development practitioners:

> For several related reasons, some historical, some inherent to the organization of development work, and some specific to particular cultural contexts, development administrations ... can be expected to have sharply gendered organizational structures, and strongly masculinized workplace cultures. (Goetz, 1992:11)

Goetz is writing here of government development administrations, but her assertion will strike a familiar chord with women working in development NG(D)Os; although the history of most such organizations, in particular their historical goal of contributing to an alternative kind of development to that promoted by government aid institutions, makes their case more complex and internally contradictory.

Some theorists take the view that certain organizational values, styles of management, ways of working are *inherently* masculine, others inherently feminine: for example, a goal- or target-oriented organizational culture is masculine, a 'nurturing' management style is feminine. Heated argument surrounds this view. Strongly contrasted styles do, to a significant extent, reflect the preferred ways of working of men and women – but not exclusively; and the suggestion that these oppositions represent innate sexual characteristics is highly debatable. We need to recognize that men and women do have different working or management styles responding not only to different views of development but to different practical and strategic needs: for instance, women may favour flexible working hours because it is they who have to juggle time at the office with domestic tasks; men's freedom from domestic tasks means they can afford rigid or demanding timetables. On the other hand, we need to avoid stereotyping: defining 'nurturing' management as feminine (or vice versa), for instance, can be seen as simply bringing private gender attributes into the public sphere once more.

What, then, does it mean to say that organizations are gendered, that their value systems, their structures, cultures and practices, their accountability and incentive systems, are gendered? It means that all these things signify something different to women and to men: women and men are situated differently in organizational structures; organizational cultures operate differently for men and women, universally favouring men over women; women's and men's work is valued differently in the organization, and may even be defined differently, with women's job descriptions, subject areas, and sometimes even management styles being defined or conditioned as extensions of their private roles and functions.

Organizations can be gendered in a number of areas.

- *Organizational ideologies and overall goals* (poverty alleviation; emergency/conflict focus; social change via economic improvement/political empowerment; etc.).[5]

- *Organizational value systems* (target-oriented vs. quality-oriented; competitive vs. cooperative; etc.).

- *Organizational structures* ('flat' vs. hierarchical; rigidly bureaucratic vs. flexible and responsive; top-down communication systems vs. more 'horizontal' ways of sharing information).

- *Management styles* ('verticalist'; efficiency-led; consultative; participatory; 'nurturing', etc.).

- *Job descriptions*, in which women staff may end up in roles which extend their domestic roles in the private sphere – e.g. being responsible for the 'soft' areas of social policy or social intervention (education, health, small income-generating projects) while men deal with the 'hard' technical or macroeconomic areas.

- *Practical arrangements*, *space and time* such as location/layout of offices; provision/design of dining rooms and lavatories; childcare provisions; working hours and their flexibility; provision of maternity paternity leave; travel requirements as part of job; etc.

- *The expression of power* (relationships between managers and staff, or male and female staff at different levels; sexual harassment).

- *Images and symbols* which tend to reproduce rather than oppose gender divisions.

## Gender, culture and diversity

What values, what 'ways of being', what underlying assumptions do we have in mind when we talk about a really gender-equal organization? How does gender interface with other forms of difference: ethnicity, economic status, age, sexuality, language, etc.? As the following two statements from *Eurostep* members illustrate, work on gender is a gateway to understanding other forms of difference and promoting diversity:

> *As a woman working in a male-dominated sector, I find that the gender issue gives me the opportunity and the strength to fight for changes that are not strictly connected with gender but which do promote the sensitivity on 'difference', in terms of age, race, ethnicity or class, which is so important for our work.*

Gender interacts with all other aspects of diversity: whatever else you are, you will also be either male or female:

> *The known, traditional, hierarchies of class, the economy, now are being diversified. Gender cuts across these divisions in a subtle, sometimes invisible way.*[6]

The contradiction between gender and 'culture' is a particular example of this. Challenging gender inequalities in counterpart organizations in a development intervention is still very often treated as unjustifiable interference in another culture, and thus as a 'crime against' diversity, in which masculine and feminine cultures should ideally be able to coexist and enrich each other.

At a theoretical level, this objection can be challenged by the view that power itself is gendered (see e.g. Acker 1992: 251: 'The links between class and race domination and gender are ubiquitous.') More concretely, Southern women themselves insist that traditional culture should not be allowed to excuse failures of gender sensitivity (various authors, *Gender and Development* 3/1, 1995), asserting that:

- a development intervention cannot leave traditional social practices untouched, nor ignore the existence of customary practice which stands in the way of development;
- culture and traditions are not fixed and immutable; they change and adapt to different external circumstances (see also Goetz 1992: 12 col 1);
- in the relationship of gender to culture, each situation is unique and specific;
- examination of both Northern and Southern assumptions about Southern cultural traditions will help us to get past gender as a no-go area.

We need to examine the extent to which, as development practitioners, we export our Northern cultural assumptions about gender roles, the sexual division of labour, and so on to the South. As Maitrayee Mukhopadhyay writes:

> *The fear that we may be imposing our own cultural values by insisting on promoting gender equity in our development work is a real one. However, it is real not because we have concerns about cultural imperialism, but because we allow our own culture-based assumptions about women to colour the way we receive alternative visions of gender equality. We assume that women in developing countries are passive and docile, and that our own view of gender roles, norms, and practices is true for everyone. We also fail to recognise the everyday forms of resistance put up by subordinated groups, because these forms of resistance may not correspond to our experience. (Maitrayee Mukhopadhyay, 'Gender relations, development practice and "culture"', Gender and Development 3/1 [Oxfam, 1995]: 15)*

This should lead us to ask the further question: what about our treatment of *Northern* cultural traditions as a no-go area? In looking at our own organizations, we find that we are often just as reluctant to upset the cultural-traditions applecart as regards gender relations, or to disturb facile but entrenched preconceptions about the relative roles of men and women, when we continue to organize job descriptions and rewards for work on the basis of this kind of supposition.

Precisely because gender relations are so engrained a part of culture, real, transformational change in gender relations of power cannot come about without cultural change. Instead of regarding cultural attitudes to gender as a no-go area for change, perhaps we should be regarding culture as the ultimate target of gender interventions. And in that case, it is with our own culture in Europe that we should be starting.

### Eurostep agencies and gender: the state of play

In this section, we look at the state of play as regards gender equality in the organizations for which we work, European development NGDOs, using them as a case study in the analysis of gender relations in organizations. The situations described here, however, have parallels in a wide variety of management relationships: for instance, the

made by their main funder, a state agency, several of the country's NGDOs had restructured and become more hierarchical and less woman-friendly, with the abandon ment of informal meeting opportunities and more restricted participation in decision-making. In the reporting agency itself, men were now doing all the public/lobbying work, women the project administration.

Nor does the presence of specific gender responsibles make progress towards internal gender equality inevitable: a number of organizations with established gender policies and staff working specifically on gender still have a majority of their female staff at administrative or assistant levels.

The debate on the advantages and disadvantages of mainstreaming is well known and still lively (see e.g. Moser, 1993: 114–18). In relation to organizational structures the mainstreaming debate seems to concentrate on the positioning of gender focal points. Participants at the workshop concluded there had been a kind of pendulum movement in the choice of structure in accord with the evolution from the WID to the GAD approach, beginning with an autonomous gender team, then introducing gender responsibles decentralized into other structures. A combination of the two strategies was felt to have produced the best results, with centralized gender focal points facilitating (external and internal) access to, and learning about, innovative practices, and decentralized focal points concentrating mainly on facilitating operationalization and implementation into the routine practice of the organization.

Almost the only point on which the experience of all agencies coincided was that there was still a great deal of lip-service paid to gender (e.g. using the agency's gender policy, or the gender balance of staff, as a public relations exercise) and a big gap between policy and practice, or even between accepting the idea of gender and the formulation of a concrete, written policy. Confronting this gap, and the double standards it encourages in the relative importance given to the promotion of gender overseas and at home, was an issue central to the concerns of this workshop.

*Eurostep* agencies continue to evince a wide variety of experiences of integrating gender into their policy and practice, and they are at very different stages on their journey towards gender-sensitive organizational development. This meant that while agencies were in relative agreement at the gender workshop about their vision of what a gender-sensitive organization would be like, it was much more difficult to arrive at a common set of strategies for making that vision a reality. In the end, each organization has to find the strategies that are appropriate for its own case and that spring organically from its own experience.

## Notes

1. See, for instance, Goetz, 1995:3; and De Beuk, 1995: no. 1, 'How to analyse organizations', which draws the analogy between an organization and a living organism or a person, highlighting its history, its context, how it relates to others, how it solves problems, its image and self-image, and its habits or ways of working.

2. Adapted from De Beuk, 1995: no. 9; Swieringa & Wierdsma, 1992: 37-44.

3. Eugenia Piza López, quoted in Kelleher et al., 1996b.

4. For these categories we are indebted to Rao and Kelleher (1995a: 71), which we have adapted slightly.

5. Goetz (1995: 5) notes that the ideologies and disciplines informing different organizations can institutionalize gender biases; she mentions research which shows that international development agencies based on disciplines of economics or agricultural economics have excluded gender differences as relevant to their focus on efficiency and growth, while organizations concerned with social and human development concerns have proven more open to the inclusion of gender issues. At the level of Northern NGDOs, a *Eurostep* staff member interviewed on gender in her agency noted that it was much harder to convince colleagues working in fields regarded as 'technical', e.g. environment and sustainable development, of the relevance of gender or social issues to their work than it was to persuade colleagues working on social and gender issues of the relevance of environmental issues.

6. Quotations are from interviews with *Eurostep* staff members; see chapter 2.

# 2 Gender dynamics within the donor organizations

In this chapter, we try to identify some issues and challenges which confront donor organizations in the donor/counterpart relationship when they begin examining gendered relations of power in their own agencies. Materials from a small survey of *Eurostep* member agencies are used as a starting point. However, when the interviews are summed up, it becomes clear that these same issues will face many, if not most organizations. In the latter half of the chapter, we turn to these more general points.

What is the situation as regards gender relations within Northern NGDOs themselves? How gender-sensitive and gender-equal are our own organizations? Have we built up the knowledge and developed the skills that would enable us to find out? These questions are directed at the relations between women and men working within European donor organizations themselves. Has an analysis of gender relations been applied to our own societies, and is that analysis reflected in the way our organizations are structured and the way people behave in them? Do the gender policies of *Eurostep* member agencies apply to their own internal organization as well as to their programmes in the South? How equal is the gender balance in our organizations in terms of staffing, decision-making structures and processes, allocation of resources? Are the roles and job descriptions of people working in the organization, and the choices open to them, constrained by gender-stereotyping? Are our organizations comfortable and supportive places for both women and men to work in? And how does the organization ensure that these matters receive attention? For instance, is it part of the job of the gender responsibles to look at questions of gender in internal organizational development as well as in programme work and relationships with counterpart organizations? Are the organizations accountable to women (Goetz, 1995: 1)? If not, why not?

We are increasingly careful, systematic and sensitive about subjecting counterpart organizations and the projects we support in the South to this kind of critical analysis of the gender relations inherent in their structures and practice. Yet, inside our own organizations, we make such an analysis far less frequently and rigorously, and this failure is reflected in the persistence, in our own organizations, of unequal gender relations that we would challenge energetically in counterpart organizations. It is still often the case that there are too few women in senior management, workplace cultures that fail to recognize women's (and men's) roles as parents and care-givers, and a generally limited and stereotyped notion of the range of choices that should be available to women; and this situation too often goes unquestioned.

As the table in chapter 1 shows, many *Eurostep* agencies see their performance on gender equality inside their own organizations as lagging behind their promotion of gender equality with counterparts. Previous *Eurostep* gender workshops pointed to this imbalance and the need to redress it. In 1993, Eugenia Piza-López wrote:

*As gender and development professionals, we will have to overcome obstacles within our own institutions .... We will have to work, within the institutional framework, on our own roles, workloads, and decision-making capacities, and particularly to address the lack of control over resources that hinders many gender specialists.*[1]

The following year, in the context of the discussion on gender and partnership, the question was posed as one of accountability to partners: the Northern NGDO 'risks losing credibility if potential partners see that more is being asked of them than the donor agency has itself achieved genderwise' (Macdonald, 1994b: 11).

In short, the gap that is to be bridged here is not only that between policy and practice in the donor agencies, but that between what donor agencies expect of their counterparts and what they expect of themselves.

## The interviews

In preparation for the 1995 *Eurostep* gender workshop, members of the network's Gender Working Group elicited the views of a variety of people working in *Eurostep* member agencies about the importance of gender in their organization and the success with which gender issues had been taken on board. Brief interviews were held with three people in each of five organizations in three countries:

- a manager (male or female) with significant influence on the gender work;
- a male colleague;
- a female colleague who is not a gender specialist.

Eight of the interviewees were women, eight men; five were managers, of whom two were women. The staff members were nearly all project or programme officers, or policy officers dealing with external policy areas such as sustainable development, AIDS, and macroeconomic issues, and thus had no specific remit to deal with internal organizational matters such as personnel or internal administration. The managers included a woman who is a former director of an NGDO, a male head of a programme department, and a male head of information whose job includes mainstreaming the gender policy within the organization.

All sixteen interviewees were asked the following questions:

- What do you find challenging and inspiring among the issues emerging from the gender debate?

- What obstacles and difficulties do you think arise from work on gender issues?

- How do you perceive your own role and responsibility with regard to gender issues both in your own agency and in your work with counterparts?

It should be noted from the outset that this was an initial exercise in sounding out the views of colleagues, with no pretensions to being definitive. The sample of interviewees is small and not comprehensive and the questions were intended to elicit only general opinions of the state of play as regards gender in the respondents' organizations. Indeed, the very incompleteness of the survey confirms the need for *Eurostep* to carry out a much more detailed analysis of the gendered relations of power in member agencies. This is a relatively new area of attention for gender change agents in development agencies, and we have yet to develop a sophisticated analysis and appropriate approaches to effecting change. These findings, therefore, should be taken as pointers to more detailed and systematic research with much wider coverage.

The responses to the three questions are summarized below.

*What do you find challenging and inspiring among the issues emerging from gender debate?*
Although the large majority of interviewees had no difficulty in identifying inspiring and challenging aspects of gender issues, the positive aspects tended to be described in idealistic and rather rhetorical terms, as aspired-to values rather than practical benefits:

> *The women's movement is a movement of a magnitude which cannot be ignored and which touches upon every corner of the globe. It is unstoppable ... the most important and effective social movement during the past decades ... proof of a capacity to actually dictate the political rules in societies. (Male manager)*

Looking at issues from a gender perspective was described as providing 'new ideas and inspiration to the debate on development and society in general'; gender analysis has helped NGDOs and partners to start thinking about 'needs that go beyond the concept of equality'.

A more realistic note was struck by a woman manager who observed that what is inspiring is not the issues involved in fighting for gender equality but the fight itself, the sense of solidarity between women, and 'the combination of strength and weakness' used by women in the struggle.

Other respondents saw the gender debate as contributing positively to women's participation in development in a general sense or as making women visible as actors in development rather than victims. Gender analysis was commonly welcomed as an enrichment of development theories and debates. It was also frequently seen as a tool: for furthering women's interests, for better target group analysis, or for analysing other forms of difference or diversity. This highlights the efficiency-oriented view of the 'added value' of gender, which appeals to many staff and managers responsible for programmes and projects in the South: 'If we want to reduce poverty in the South we have to support women' (male manager).

> *The best resources are to be found among women: women have experience (as caretakers of households, children, they know how to save money, etc.) that can*

*be used in communities and organizations for common goals. Women are able to concentrate on serious tasks, are more committed than men. (Male manager)*

Only one programme officer (male) explicitly named the empowerment of women through training, capacity and leadership building, and awareness-raising as a challenge.

Women interviewees in particular found the gender debate supportive and inspiring in their own work. Some felt that both the GAD approach and the women's movement had contributed much to their own personal and professional development and understanding; for others a particularly positive aspect was that work on gender gave them a sense of real partnership and unity with women in the South: 'gender is my own cause too.'

*Gender issues, in a male-dominated sector, give me the opportunity and the strength to fight for changes that are not strictly connected with gender but promote sensitivity to differences. (Female manager)*

Only two people (from the same organization) did not feel any particular challenge or inspiration in their organization as a result of the gender debate.

*What obstacles and difficulties do you think arise from work on gender issues?*
In contrast to the challenges and inspirations, interviewees described obstacles and constraints in a much more down-to-earth, practical way, and often in more detail. Here, too, respondents were more prepared to reveal and defend their reluctance to take gender issues fully into account. However, with the exception of very general features such as 'male chauvinism' and the gap between the ideal and the possible, almost all the obstacles and difficulties identified referred chiefly if not exclusively to work with counterparts. Only one respondent, a male department head, mentioned underrepresentation of women at senior management level as an obstacle. However, several warned against the tendency to misrepresent gender as meaning nothing more than the achievement of gender parity on the organization's staff. The obstacles and difficulties identified fell into five broad categories.

*Ignorance or misunderstanding of what gender is about.* Interviewees noted that 'in our society, the concept of gender as a difference is still not fully understood' (female manager); 'gender is usually seen as just another word for women' (female programme officer). Much resistance can be disguised as mystification or ignorance, or as 'gender fatigue' – the claim that the debate can be 'boring' or counterproductive, or that it has now been sufficiently dealt with and no longer needs particular attention. On the other hand, the need to map gender relations onto country- or culture-specific political and economic analyses was identified.

An associated problem is the continuing tendency to treat gender as an 'add-on' rather than an intrinsic feature of every development issue, and consequently to feel that gender considerations generate extra work; that gender 'represents an additional concern and adds work in conditions that are usually hard' (female project officer); that gender work is 'time-consuming' and requires 'yet another demanding micro-level investigation during project appraisal' (male staff member). Such responses confirm that the challenge identified by one respondent, a female policy adviser, of integrating the gender analysis so that it is not merely an appendix (but an appendix heavily burdened with guilt, as we will see below) is still a very real one in many agencies and reveal the defensiveness many people, both male and female, still feel as soon as the issue of gender is raised.

More than one respondent thought there was still a tendency to view women in the South as victims, and that this was counterproductive. A female policy adviser felt the lack of hard economic data to support gendered analyses that show women's productivity, etc.; she felt that arguments urging awareness of the consequences of development interventions for women still tended to rest on principles of charity and 'kindness'.

*Cultural resistance by partners and donors' reluctance to question it.* This was perhaps the problem most frequently mentioned, but it was nearly always couched in terms of the donor/counterpart relationship and the resistance on the part of the counterpart. Resistance to recognizing and addressing unequal gender relations within the donor organization itself was hardly ever referred to. Here is a fairly typical response:

> *The main problem is the great difference in cultural sensitiveness that exists between us and our partners as far as gender is concerned. Even women are not aware of the existence of the issue in most cases ... This puts us, European, rich and 'donors,' in a delicate position. (Male project officer)*

There was concern that 'Western concepts still dominate', and that Northern agencies, by 'imposing' their approach to gender issues, invited lip-service and tokenism on the part of counterpart organizations. Lack of interest in gender issues was generally imputed to counterparts, and particularly male staff in counterparts, rather than to staff in donor organizations. One respondent had found that men in counterpart organizations think allocating resources to gender work is 'useless' (although less resistance is encountered with beneficiaries). While this is obviously an important and delicate issue, it is significant that only one interviewee (female) mentioned that European men feel threatened by discussion of gender issues, and it is tempting to speculate that displacing resistance to gender issues largely onto *counterpart* organizations may be in part a tactic for coping with the anxiety the theme still seems to provoke in Northern NGDOs.

There was awareness that the change necessary to overcome this kind of resistance is principally one of organizational culture, but few suggestions as to how to promote this kind of change. On the contrary, the lack of 'tools' to address the problem, or inability to use existing planning, monitoring and evaluation tools from a gender perspective, was frequently cited as an obstacle.

*Gaps between rhetoric and real practice.* Different aspects of this problem were mentioned several times, particularly by women interviewees. They include lip-service, tokenism, failure to take gender arguments seriously in 'technical' contexts such as sustainable development, failure by men in the South to take women from the donor organization seriously, and so on. 'Gender is still a new issue, accepted in theory but not in practice,' said one female project officer. Another woman project officer drew attention to the discrepancy between the public behaviour of leaders of women's organizations in the South, 'who in public take a radical stand in the name of their organization', and their more traditional behaviour vis-à-vis husbands/partners and children in their domestic roles. (Similar contradictory behaviour among women managers in Northern agencies was not mentioned.)

A male manager expressed this contradiction at a general level as 'the continuing dilemma of what one wants and what is possible ... the tension between continuity and change', where there are legitimate arguments on both sides. This manager noted that his own organization would like to have gender parity among the staff in terms both of numbers and positions, but that the space for manoeuvre was limited. The struggle for gender equality is not happening in isolation but alongside and interwoven with other required performances and conditions.

*The slowness of change.* This was seen as both frustrating and inevitable. It was felt that changing attitudes and cultures on gender issues is not a short-term goal: 'training is not enough, we must be prepared to wait for a long time until gender becomes a "natural" component of our work' (female manager). One manager (male) thought gender specialists expected change to happen too quickly and stressed that development takes time.

*Women and power.* Some interviewees, mostly women, illustrated the uneasy relationship women have with power. This was the point at which issues of internal organizational development arose most clearly. A female manager felt that the nature of feminist management has not yet been clearly defined, and that – in the absence of any other model – women have internalized masculine patterns of management. This produces internal conflicts both in the individual and her group when a woman manager is operating in an unfriendly environment where she is in the minority.

Self-righteousness and extreme ideological positions within the women's movement were criticized as counterproductive. On the other hand, it was noted that 'fear of feminism' could create a situation where any confrontation with another woman would be interpreted as a 'cold war' between feminist and anti-feminist ideologies, regardless of whether gender was the issue actually at stake. This feeling of threat surfaced also in the view that a continued focus by feminists on changing 'male-dominated structures' was 'rather conservative'. (Male manager)

*How do you perceive your own role and responsibility with regard to gender issues both in your own agency and in your work with counterparts?*

Responses to this question obviously varied with the respondent's formal position within the organization (as manager, programme/project officer, policy officer, etc.) as well as with their sex, and with the degree of power they perceived themselves to command in the organization – which is not directly correlated with their formal position. Size of organization did not seem to have a very significant effect on the responsibilities people assumed for promotion of gender sensitivity. But it emerged clearly that nearly all interviewees saw themselves as change agents of one kind or another, rather than as simply carrying out a policy handed to them from elsewhere. Respondents described their roles and responsibilities in terms of:

- promoting information-sharing, non-sexist language, appropriate rules in the organization;
- allocating resources;
- increasing the numerical participation of women at all levels in projects;
- demanding accountability from counterparts and own organization;
- raising the question of gender carefully with counterparts;
- sensitizing colleagues and counterparts to the gender aspects of cross-cutting issues such as human rights, AIDS, sustainable development;
- mainstreaming gender policy in the organization;
- confronting male colleagues with gender-sensitive solutions;
- influencing the integration of gender into country programmes at policy level;
- keeping the debate going and establishing dialogue with counterparts;
- promoting networking and creating broad spaces of consensus, to get an organization to accept changes.

The majority of these activities can apply equally to work with counterparts and within the donor organization itself. However, it was managers more often than staff who drew the links between internal organizational development and programme work (see below); although one woman staff member, a policy adviser, was very explicit about such links:

> *For me the questions of human rights and democracy also apply to the internal functioning of an organization, and thus there is a need for gender equality within an organization.*

Project and programme officers saw their role as more counterpart-oriented: assessing projects for gender sensitivity, integrating gender policy into country programmes, and dialoguing with counterparts. They stressed their responsibility for informing counterparts about gender issues and encouraging them to recognize that taking gender on board is in their own interest, not just that of the donor, and that it is a long-term benefit for future generations. Few interviewees mentioned as a responsibility raising issues of gender equality with colleagues; however, one head of department felt the

## GENDER ISSUES IN INTERNAL ORGANIZATIONAL DEVELOPMENT

The following issues concerning gender and internal organizational development were mentioned in one or more of the interviews. They are clearly applicable to organizations in general, not just to donor NGDOs:

- the gendered nature of power, and the power-related aspects of diversity;
- the positive achievement signified by the institutionalization of gender in organizations;
- the need to take gender into account as a factor in political and economic analyses;
- the continuing need to sensitize people in the organization to the gender aspects of human rights, AIDS, environment, and other 'horizontal' issues, and technical issues (it is easier to interest gender specialists in technical issues than vice versa);
- the importance of raising the profile of gender in an organization for supporting, strengthening, and increasing the awareness of women working in it;
- male chauvinism, especially in its various disguises;
- women's internalization of male patterns of behaviour, particularly in management; 'feminist management' remains undefined;
- underrepresentation of women, particularly in technical jobs, and limited space for manoeuvre around gender parity (especially in an organization where there are few management or policy jobs);
- the multiple workload borne by gender specialists, especially in smaller organizations, because gender is at best treated as equal to other policy areas in terms of staff time allocation, rather than being recognized as an element present in all policy areas;
- recognition of the double responsibilities of private and working lives for both men and women;
- the slowness of change, tension between the impulse towards change and organizational inertia; the contradiction between what is desired and what is possible;
- overreliance on 'tools': the search for emotionally neutral, technical solutions to problems which deal essentially with ideology, attitude and organizational culture;
- the direct relationship between gender equality and high-quality performance;
- the effectiveness of affirmative action.

policy officer said she had not had time to develop a detailed gender analysis because her job required quick responses too often.

Managers more often (but not exclusively) drew the links between the organization itself and its Southern counterparts. One manager saw very clearly the same dilemmas applying to the South and the Northern NGDO itself; for instance, the struggle for gender equality, however urgent and justifiable, is not the only struggle, and does not occur in a vacuum.

Managers were also aware of the *realpolitik* aspects of promoting what has become a high-profile issue in recent years. More than one manager remarked that a visible commitment to gender quality was good for the organization's image.

However, few of the managers interviewed actually talked about issues relating to gender *and management*, or to the specific problems of being or becoming a gender-sensitive manager. On the other hand, staff members did talk about the problems of being a gender-sensitive programme or project officer – but again this was mostly with reference to their roles as appraisers, evaluators, etc. of the gender content of projects and the gender awareness of counterparts. Some staff members referred to their dialogue with colleagues on gender, for instance in confronting technically-oriented male colleagues with gender-sensitive solutions, making them aware of the complexity of social issues.

Finally, the interviews reveal that managers in many cases evinced a deeper and more sensitive awareness of gender issues, and a greater commitment to gender equality, than female staff members, pointing to a need for continued training and sensitization of both male and female staff and a continued commitment to providing resources for this. Some of the important issues that came up in the interviews are summarized in the box.

## Bringing gender back home

While they talked in detail about issues of promoting gender sensitivity and gender equality with counterparts, interviewees did not talk in any but the most general terms about the extent to which their organizations had succeeded in 'getting the institution right for women', as Anne Marie Goetz (1995) puts it. In chapter 5, below, we identify some features that would characterize a gender-sensitive organization – an organization that would be right for women. Goetz (ibid.) summarizes some of the broad principles that must inform an organization if it is to be right for women: for instance, accountability to women, non-gender-stereotyped roles and choices for women as well as men at all levels of power in the organization, an organizational culture which values and utilizes women's perspectives and allows expression of their interests.

However, the *Eurostep* interviewees did not often refer to these kinds of criteria as a gauge of the gender-fairness of their own organizations, nor include their absence among the obstacles they have encountered. The analysis devoted to identifying whose interests are served by a programme in the South and whose interests are dominant in the Southern NGO with whom the donor organization is cooperating does not seem to

NGDO organizational culture of self-sacrifice and self-exploitation leads people to feel they should not worry about what happens inside the organization, only about what happens 'in the field'. They tend not to question whether the organization serves the interests of its workers at all, for the ideology of development organizations is that they exist to serve the interests of people in the developing world. But this tendency could also indicate discomfort with the idea of bringing the issue home to roost and applying to one's own workplace, one's own management structures and organizational culture, attitudes of one's own colleagues, the same analysis as is applied to counterpart organizations safely distanced by geography, culture and a funding relationship in which the donor organization is clearly the more powerful partner.

Reflection on gender in our own internal development is in one way less complex than such reflection with regard to counterparts, because we have only our own policy to cope with, and our own, familiar culture and value systems. At the same time, it is a good deal less comfortable, because we are no longer looking at something that is happening 'out there', 'in the field', and at a relationship in which we are by far the most powerful party. Our own culture and values are at issue, our own personalities and personal relationships with people close to us at work (and often people with more power than we have, since gender advisers usually have a consultative rather than a decision-making capacity in NGDOs) are involved.

These questions carry an emotional freight. In this context, it is impossible to consider the interviewees' replies as totally objective. They are inevitably weighted with the feelings of the respondents, which may spring from their own sense of power or powerlessness in their organization. They will also be conditioned by the relationship between respondent and questioner: in this case the interviewers were members of their organization's gender teams, and this may have drawn out overly politically correct responses ('tell her what she wants to hear') or, on the other hand, defensive responses from those who felt attacked by discussions of gender relations, as well as the more thought-out observations from those who support the gender team and its work. The same set of questions, asked by a male manager, would probably generate answers which were very differently weighted in terms of enthusiasm, resistance, and honesty: in that situation feminists might be the ones to feel under threat and therefore to express their support of gender in over-idealistic terms; waverers, unsure of how a positive response might be received and how disapproval might affect their own chances in the organization, might conceal their true support for gender; while resisters might feel less constrained in expressing their opposition.

Analysing gender-based power relations inside our own workplaces and with our own colleagues is far more painful and emotionally demanding – even threatening – than analysing those relations as they apply to a counterpart organization in the South. Our own fears and uncertainties, identities, including sexual identities, and personal relationships come under the microscope. Moreover, many people feel 'guilt-tripped' by discussions of gender. Gender responsibles themselves may have to bear some of the blame for this: gender justice can seem to us so blindingly obvious a prerequisite for true development that we may sometimes fail to recognize how closely the issue of gender touches on personal feelings and anxieties and may 'push' gender aggressively and insensitively. Making people feel guilty merely pushes them further towards resistance.

But there may be a deeper reason, to do with the gendered nature of power. Gender is the primary difference in human society, intersecting with all other differences. Whatever else we are, we are all either male or female and, as such, locked into a gendered hierarchy of power which – from our own personal point of view – we will have very differing degrees of interest in changing. Even more than reminding us of our own racism if we are white, working in development reminds us of our own sexism if we are men, or (in a more complex way) if we are women who have managed – as most of us have – to come to a more or less satisfactory accommodation with the male-dominated world. And we may also not feel powerful enough to do anything to change those gender relations of power. If you feel powerless as a woman in your own life, you may feel incapable, as a development worker, of changing the gender power balance for any other women; or, on the other hand, you may feel angry that your work somehow empowers you to change the balance for other women but not for yourself. If you are a man working in a development agency, committed to equalities of all kinds, and you recognize that you have power not only over women (and men) in counterpart organizations but also over women (and possibly other men) in your own organization, you may feel guilty about your own power. But you may also feel powerless in relation to many of the structures you are working to change: national and supranational governments, international financial institutions, global corporations and trading blocs. The vast power of these institutions can make you feel puny both as an individual and as a member of a small and relatively poor organization. Development work teaches us that power is fragile; those who have a small amount of it – and are confident that they are using it for good purposes – may resent having to surrender any of it, even in the interest of a greater justice.

These feelings may not necessarily be conscious; indeed, they may be deeply buried and for that reason all the more painful to unearth. But talking about gender inevitably reminds us at some level of our own – usually uneasy – position on the gendered power scale and the double binds involved in analysing that position and acting accordingly. We need to recognize that extreme reactions of 'political correctness' or defensive dismissal of gender issues highlight the emotional risk to which people feel exposed when discussing the power relations of which they are a part.

> ... still men feel threatened and insecure when a gender debate starts, even on theoretical grounds. They don't dare to object, but they feel embarrassed and they try to overcome this by joking, drawing attention to more 'neutral' aspects, etc. (Female manager)

## Power, role and personality

As we have remarked already, society is gendered, and it is almost universally gendered so as to favour males. This pattern of power relations has been constructed and reinforced throughout history to the point where, just by virtue of being male or female, each human being is slotted, virtually at birth, into a gendered hierarchy of power: males at the top, females at the bottom. Almost immediately, however, other differences come into play, defining more precisely the person's position in the pyramid of power: at the individual level, their age, their appearance, their physical size and strength, their mental ability, their economic and cultural status or that of their families. Then their position is further influenced by the kind of society of which they are members: its wealth or poverty, its stability or instability, its rigidity or flexibility, the kinds of diversity it allows or suppresses. These factors interact with each other and with the person's gender to define the extent of their power in relation to other women and men in different arenas in their own and other societies. Finally, all these aspects of power both influence and are influenced by our individual personalities.

This may all sound self-evident, but it is worth recalling when we are analysing the responses individual people give to questions about gender in their own organizations – that is, in their own daily working lives. Perceptions of the gender debate and its value will vary not only according to the respondent's sex but also to his or her age, ethnicity, etc., and according to where s/he feels s/he is placed in the organization's pyramid of power. Remember, too, that how powerful we are and how powerful we feel are not necessarily the same thing.

Attitudes to the promotion of gender equality (or any change to improve diversity) in an organization may be influenced by a wide range of factors, including:
- theoretical gender analysis, whether based on welfare, equity, empowerment, etc.;
- ideological commitment (feminism, but not only feminism);
- personal conviction and experience;
- expectations and standards (what is considered a satisfactory level of gender integration?);
- concern with the image of the organization (rather than convictions);
- to whom the person is and feels accountable;
- pragmatism, desire for efficiency;
- fear, guilt, shame, embarrassment;
- enlightened self-interest;
- unenlightened self-interest!

Different kinds of people in an organization will have different ways of promoting or defending their own group or individual interests according to their personalities as well as their role, status and power within the organization. For instance, the Norwegian researcher Ann Lotherington, analysing reactions to the introduction of gender issues into an organization, classified reactions according to four types of people, each of which may include both women and men:
- innovators: people who cut across the male/female divide, who are
- loyal bureaucrats: people who will go along with any policy as long as they are provided with the tools to implement it, and who see no need to question anything that comes from above;

- hesitators: people who will support a new policy in public, because it is necessary to be seen to go with the organization's latest trends; possibly careerists; people who care about the organization's image;
- tough guys: the strongest and most explicit opponents, most dangerous and difficult when in positions of leadership.[2]

Similarly, we can identify different types among people who act as change agents on gender, who will have different roles to play and different effects depending on where they are located in the organization and what kind of person they are. The diagram in table 2, adapted from a schema first developed by De Beuk in 1994, can be used as a matrix to illuminate the many patterns and processes that may be occurring successively or simultaneously in an organization's process of change as regards gender. It represents a possible typology identifying typical attitudes or responses to be expected among different groups at different points in the change process. The vertical arrows represent the temporal progression from the beginning of the change process to its later stages.

This schema identifies typical responses of change agents operating in organizations with different levels of commitment to gender equality.

- The lone pioneer: starts from a position of keen awareness of injustice and women's gender disadvantage. May feel that nothing will ever change, but becomes a change agent, paradoxically, through this passive position. Makes no impact on the dominant (management) group, but may attract the main subdominant (employee) group, who identify with her expressions of powerlessness and are led to begin analysing power.

- The fighter: turns her anger into action. Both challenges and impresses the dominant group, and may make them feel guilty, but is likely therefore to provoke strong resistance from them. The vanguard for gender, a risk-taker. She may be seen as a champion by the main employee group, but they may be reticent about expressing support of her views for fear of alienating the more powerful members of the organization.

- The player: is diplomatic, pragmatic; builds alliances, strategizes, negotiates; allies with the dominant group, appealing to their self-interest and to their interest in the overall quality of the organization and its work. May suffer internal conflict because of the need to compromise on her personal conviction in order to achieve the achievable, and may risk cooption by the dominant group.

All three types are necessary and valuable contributors, at different moments, to the gender learning process in organizations. Their responses and personality types may exist alongside each other. While the fighter may not make an impression (or at least not a favourable one) on the dominant group, she will sow seeds of doubt, create spaces, and take risks that allow players and other women in the organization to come

**Table 2  Typical models and responses in a dynamic process of organizational change**

| Gender status in organizations | Typical response of management/ dominant group | Typical response of other employees/ subdominant group | Typical model of change agent | Typical strategies of change agents |
|---|---|---|---|---|
| *Gender-blind*: no recognition of gender differentials; assumptions include biases in favour of existing gender relations ↓ | Defensive; easily accused; insulated by power ↓ | Passive; lacks awareness ↓ | *The lone pioneer:* frequently stigmalized; feels victimized; sometimes like a frozen rabbit; needs support base ↓ | Putting gender on the agenda by explaining; giving facts and figures; formal/informal organizing ↓ |
| *Gender-aware:* recognition of gender differentials but no, or fragmented, translation into practice ↓ | Feels attacked ; intimidated; sometimes overly impressed and eager to be 'politically correct' ↓ | Increasingly aware but afraid to rock the boat; others who feel threatenned by change turn the change agent into a lightning rod ↓ | *The fighter:* charismatic, fast moving; risk-taker; not afraid of conflict; has a small support base in the organization ↓ | Arguments based on ideology and values; forms strategic alliances (inside and outside the organization) ↓ |
| *Gender- redistributive:* interventions intended to transform existing distributions to create a more balanced relationship between women and men | Cares about the organiza- tional gender image; is interested in making alliances with change agents; needs support in policy development and implemen- tation ↓ | Prepared to support management; in need of skills and tools to bring policies into practice ↓ | *The player:* tries to 'play' the organiza- tion; recognizes opportunities; negotiates; is diplomatic, flexible ↓ | Building planning, monitoring and evaluation systems; mechanisms for learning and accountability; promotion of innovative practices; outside networking |

forward more confidently. The fighter and the player together can persuade the dominant group to change. The lone pioneer and the fighter can raise the awareness of the subdominant group. As this group becomes more aware, they will probably become first pioneers (aware of inequality) and then fighters (angry about it).

As these remarks suggest, the schema above is a very flexible one. The diagram looks linear, but in reality the interconnections, alliances, progressions over time, lines of influence are much more complex. Viewing the diagram as an illustration of processes over time, for instance, we might find that people move along the vertical axis, as indicated by the arrows. Even this in itself is of course not a linear progression, emotionally speaking, but more a pendulum, swinging between two extreme reactions and finally coming to rest at a midpoint – a progression possibly from the least useful to the most useful approach as far as negotiating change is concerned. The arrows can also represent a learning process at all three levels, with the employee group moving from unawareness to strategic awareness and the management group moving from a defensive position to one of enlightened self-interest and a perception of the common stake in gender equality.

Also at work will be processes of influence and pressure. Opinion leaders in the organization will exert pressure and influence both upward and downward. In the dominant group this may produce feelings of being attacked (by the fighters) or accused (by the pioneers), and responses of defensiveness, protectiveness of their own interests and positions, guilt, as they are attacked by the fighters, and so on. Downward influence on the main subdominant group could be educative, drawing-out, consciousness-raising, and so on.

The structure and procedures, but especially the culture, of the organization will determine to some extent what kinds of people are allowed to operate and with what degree of freedom, which strategies work, how much space there is for each type.

Among typical kinds of arguments used by the different change agents in pressing for gender sensitivity and equality, we can distinguish three main levels:

- the level of *facts*: basing arguments on empirical knowledge of women's inequality and the personal experience of the proponent of the argument, appealing to the interlocutor's sense of identification with the problem;
- the level of *morals*, *ideology*, *values*: arguing that the organization must embrace gender equality because it is morally right. This approach, while clearly supported by ordinary morality, can provoke insincere politically correct responses or alternatively defensiveness from people who feel guilt-tripped by it;
- the level of *efficiency* and *pragmatism*: putting forward evidence to prove that things work better if gender relations are equal, adducing evidence such as women's more efficient use of credit, better work done by employees who are parents if the workplace has on-site childcare, etc. Appeals to enlightened self-interest of decision-makers in the organization.

Here too, of course, exact correlation cannot be made between arguments, their proponents and their targets. Gender change agents tend in debate to switch from one to the other; at one time or another all these arguments and more have been used to argue

Southern counterpart organizations' failure to understand what the donor means by 'gender', especially if the donor itself is using the term too loosely;

- accountability: the more powerful partner must be prepared to listen to, and if appropriate act on, criticism from the less powerful;
- the need to analyse in advance, as far as possible, what changes an intervention will produce: not just the intended changes but the unintentional side effects – such as a change in the gender balance;
- the role of external agents (usually brought in by the more powerful partner) and the effects of their actions. In North/South relationships this can be a point where gender hierarchies intersect with the North/South division of power.

The case studies illustrate a wide range of problems that can arise in work on gender issues in the donor/counterpart relationship and reveal a number of needs. Some of these are:

- failure to take account of women's needs and interests from the start (case study 2);
- the dangers of imposing a policy or a procedure, or of not openly recognizing differences in priorities between donor and counterpart when negotiating agreement, possibly leading to lip-service on gender (case study 2);
- the counterproductive effects of tokenism, which can effectively bring progress on gender to a halt (case study 1);
- too slow or too fast a pace of change, or external imposition of deadlines;
- an unfavourable external political or economic climate (case study 1);
- men's insecurity about gender issues (case study 4);
- the continuing dilemma between setting up separate activities for women or integrating women's interests into mainstream activities (case study 2) – although separate activities open space for women to gain experience, self-confidence and visibility, their empowerment is very limited if the women's programmes are not given access to mainstream resourcing;
- the personalities and influence of programme staff, and other interpersonal relations (often, but not necessarily, gender-based) (case study 4);
- rivalry over resources between all-male or male-dominated and women-only groups (case study 2);
- parallels (and tensions) between approaches to gender-based discrimination or oppression and that based on other forms of difference, such as ethnicity (case studies 3, 4);
- the need for concrete and practical tools for working on gender that address behaviour and attitude change and lead to real changes in practice (case study 4);
- the need for gender training to be participatory, to involve men in positive ways, and to link in with other trainings and activities (case study 4).

Factors influencing success, on the other hand, include the greater acceptablility to counterparts of an inclusive gender approach rather than a women-only WID approach; dialogue aimed at encouraging men to recognize their self-interest in gender equality; and, sometimes, upward pressure on the NGO counterpart from the target group.

As readers will find, some of the interventions described were perceived to be successful, others unsuccessful. But who defines what is a success or a failure? Also, successes and failures are seldom unalloyed, and valuable lessons can be learned from even the most disappointing situations. It is perhaps useful to see success and failure not as two opposed poles but as points on a spectrum of possible impacts. Most 'successes' contain limitations, and most 'failures' have some positive aspects. How do we define a successful intervention? At what point (in a process which is seldom strictly linear) do the positive results outweigh the negative, or vice versa? If we judge the success of an intervention in the broad sense, by whether it meets women's practical and strategic gender needs,[1] this can obviously be achieved in very varying degrees (and the goal can be interpreted in very different ways). A key indicator might be how far the intervention has contributed to increasing women's range of options and choices and to transcending gender-stereotyped concepts of those options; but this too is only one of a variety of possible indicators. At the end of the day, the degree of success of a gender intervention can be measured only in terms of the specific context, expectations, possibilities and constraints applying to each counterpart or project.

## A progressive but male-dominated organization

*Situation and context.* This case study concerns a cultural organization in South Asia which was started by a group of journalists, artists, and writers from different ethnic groups to offer a counterbalance to the repressive political and cultural climate prevailing in their country. The main objective of this counterpart organization is to organize an alternative cultural sector to the state-dominated ideological cultural sector, on the one hand, and the commercial sector, on the other. Its main activities are supporting grassroots organizations by implementing cultural programmes, translating literature to encourage inter-ethnic cultural exchanges, and organizing seminars and workshops to that end.

In 1994 the organization had 11 paid staff, of whom two were women (programme staff). There is a committee of 12, all men, and about 50 volunteers, of whom 15 are women. They cooperate closely with a women's NGO working on culture which is active in the region.

An evaluation team which analysed this organization with regard to gender concluded that, although the organization explicitly upholds the idea of gender equality and there is cooperation with women's NGOs, the organization itself is male-dominated, not only in numbers but also in its culture. The organizational culture has its origins in the activist left-wing movement, and although women participate in the programmes, they find it difficult to gain access to decision-making in the organization, which is dominated by men. There is a women's programme, but it is not successful and has no influence on the main programmes.

Nevertheless, this intervention was not simply negative; any intervention has positive (side?) effects as well. In this case, these were:

- an increased awareness and need to debate gender issues further and to fine-tune procedures currently available;
- an explicit commitment to learn from what happened and an appreciation that individual staff members' perspectives do relate to their own life experiences;
- a critical attitude towards gender training and the need to share this with counterpart organizations in the region which provide gender training.

## Some conclusions

While, at one level, every situation and its external context is different and demands a specific, even a tailored, strategy, there are also common features in the case studies that allow some general observations.

### Donor power

The question of power is fundamental to an analysis of what makes a successful gender intervention, in particular as a gender intervention aims to facilitate a process of women's empowerment. People with power do not usually tend to analyse or criticize it; but, as the people who hold the purse-strings in development cooperation, donor agencies have a serious responsibility to recognize their own power and to analyse its effects – deliberate and unintended, positive and negative – on the counterparts with whom they interact.

The decision to impose a policy on a counterpart, or to make meeting certain standards a condition for receiving assistance, clearly raises ethical questions. What justifies us in thinking we can (or must) change other people? And once we decide as donors that we have a right to change other people, and even to stimulate them to change by offering or withholding resources (conditionality), how do we cope with the resultant problems of transparency, accountability and manipulation? Most donor organizations are familiar with the situation in which a counterpart organization, or a sector within it, pays lip-service to donor-led ideas, such as gender equality – promising compliance to secure funding which may be conditional on its accepting such ideas, but ignoring them in practice. This is a risk which is almost built into any cooperation relationship involving funding, and donor agencies do have to recognize that counterparts, perhaps rebelling against their own dependency, may parry the financial power of the donor with the only power they feel they have, the power to make false promises.

On the other hand, there are limits to negotiation. Donors do have the right to draw a bottom line or set minimum standards, according to their basic principles – and if the counterpart disagrees with the donor at this basic level, then there is little point to the partnership, on either side. But Southern counterparts are obviously under more acute constraints than Northern donors, and are therefore less free to draw *their* bottom lines firmly. However, often these bottom lines (on either side) are not made sufficiently clear at the start of the relationship, for a variety of reasons. Counterparts, understandably anxious not to endanger a source of funding, may be vague about exactly how seriously they have taken gender issues on board or are prepared or able to do so at the current stage in their development. Donors may not have been specific enough as to what outcome they hoped to see: for instance (in the case studies in this chapter), more women in decision-making positions in the counterpart organization; a higher, or qualitatively different, participation of women in the organization; a change in the gendered division of labour or of management responsibilities; securing funding for a feminist organization. Donor objectives such as 'empowerment of women', 'meeting women's practical and strategic needs' or 'increased gender sensitivity' may need to be expressed in more tangible, measurable terms and defined in culture-specific ways: 'increased empowerment of women' means something very different in an African small farmers' union and a Latin American popular education institute. How are 'women's practical and strategic needs' defined in each context? If the donor expects a qualitative rather than a quantitative change, how is the change to be measured?

In short, it is essential for donor agencies to be both specific and transparent, from the outset, about their expectations and the minimum standards of practice they find acceptable, and for counterpart organizations to be equally honest and transparent about the extent to which they feel they can fulfil what is being asked of them and about the constraints they foresee.

Conditionality is inherent in all aid-giving: the very process of preparing a project proposal according to guidelines set by the donor is an exercise in meeting conditions. It is our responsibility to be sensitive to this. There is a delicate balance between sensitivity to counterparts' needs, capabilities, and constraints (for instance, we should be aware that the timescales of donors and counterparts may be very different: donors want quick results, counterparts move much more slowly) and acquiescence in the perpetuation of unjust and unequal structures in the name of culture or tradition.

As soon as we give aid, as well as wielding our own power we inevitably change the power balance (including the gender balance) in the counterpart organization. Whom do we choose to empower, and how do we choose them? Is our partnership with the women, the men, or both the women and the men working within an organization and represented by it? This raises the question of *stakeholders* in a development intervention, a category which embraces a larger group than simply counterparts. The directors of a counterpart NGO may think that setting minimum standards of gender sensitivity is an imposition or an interference by the donor; but staff members in the NGO, or people in the target group who are the ultimate beneficiaries, may welcome it and see the common interest in gender equality between them and the donor as a potential strategic alliance that can influence the intermediary organization. A triangular dialogue – a trialogue – between donor, counterpart and target group may be a useful strategy.

Moreover, it is impossible to separate the personal issues of attitude change as regards power from the organizational ones, because attitude change is part of organizational culture, which involves the feelings, fears and prejudices of others. When a 'powerful' Northern gender officer – a woman – makes demands or sets conditions on men in the counterpart organization, who may be the most powerful players in their own organization but are less powerful than she is, this can be very threatening to the men's self-image and to the image they want to purvey in their own societies. Personal fears are activated, fears that touch something far deeper for them than merely the loss of organizational prestige involved in surrendering some of their power and privilege to women (and in doing so, to appear to bow to the will of a foreign woman). What the men fear is an attack on their masculinity, their identity as men.

One strategy that has met with some success is that of Puntos de Encuentro in Nicaragua, which carries out gender training with men, not in technical terms but around awareness, starting from the men's own experience of masculinity. Male facilitators work with groups of men from all walks of life: farmers, teachers, young men, policemen, etc. Gender training with women routinely starts with this kind of work, with looking at what it means to be a woman; but these men had never been invited to talk about their own lives as men. Thus their deep fears about changing long-established gender relations had not been addressed, so that gender interventions met with firm resistance.

Gender sensitivity training with both men and women may be a useful strategy. At the same time, it appears that men, like most dominant groups, find it difficult to analyse their own dominance.


## Gender interventions do not exist in a vacuum

It should be clear that work on promoting gender awareness and gender equality cannot be introduced in a vacuum, since gender relations are intricately woven through the whole set of cultural, economic, and political relations that define not only the context in which the counterpart is operating but the relationship between donor and counterpart. Recognizing this helps us to recognize that, in a complex situation where the unequal relationship between men and women is one of the problems, it may not always be the only one, or the determinant one. All too common is the situation where people are getting poorer because of structural adjustment and there is very fierce competition for increasingly scarce resources, to the extent that men and women in a community are actually competing for aid. The problem is not just about gender; it is also about global and national economic forces, impoverishment, frustration; but these are all gendered and impact on women and men in different ways, reflecting gender roles and relations.

So, *all* the factors impacting on a community or a counterpart organization must be analysed by both donor and counterpart before an intervention is made. Gender is not one of a set of issues, it is an element of all issues. For instance, increasing awareness of the feminization of poverty has made it easier for NGDO staff to convince colleagues of the importance of gender; but there is a danger that this may be interpreted narrowly as a need to focus on income-generating projects for women, which, though they may meet women's practical gender needs, do not necessarily address their strategic gender needs, and do not recognize the *interdependence* of women's and men's roles and positions in a society.

This understanding that gender is *in* every issue is fundamental to an understanding of the interaction between gender and culture. Case study 1 (the South-Asian cultural organization) illustrates a problem frequently encountered in work on gender issues in organizations with a history of activism, usually on the left. Such organizations tend to be male-dominated and masculine in their culture: they interpret gender equality in terms only of equal opportunities, not of affirmative action, and they see gender as secondary to the struggle for other values (national liberation, democratization, social justice in general, class or racial equality). They may even believe that once their 'primary' goal has been accomplished, gender relations will somehow equalize themselves automatically. How can a donor help such organizations to recognize that gender equality is not consequent upon democratization (for instance), but is *part of* democratization?

In politically active organizations, in the South just as in the North, gender struggles may be part of the political struggles within the organization. Yet, when donor organizations begin gender interventions of the kind seen in these case studies, they often do so without first making a sufficient analysis of the internal political dynamics of the counterpart organization, including its gender dynamics. It is not surprising that such interventions have only limited success, for if the organization making the intervention is not fully aware of the existing struggles for gender equality within the counterpart organization, or of the state of the debates and struggles around gender issues in the counterpart's country at large, it has no really firm analytical basis on which to rest its intervention.

On the other hand, if the donor analyses the gender relations and gender struggles in the counterpart and its external context – and even more if it supports such a self-analysis on the part of the counterpart – it will be facilitating a positive process of recognition of the links between gender struggles and other political struggles, not only within the counterpart and in the donor/counterpart relationship but more broadly, opening the way for the building of mutually strengthening alliances on gender issues. The importance of such linkages can be seen in the example from ¡Somos Amigos!

The pace of change, too, is not necessarily determined only by gender-related factors such as the degree of commitment or reluctance to change on the part of the organization or the effectiveness of the change agent. It often depends on factors quite external to the organization: for instance, when donors are impatient (perhaps because of their own cultural expectations, which they may unwittingly impose on the counterpart) or when a donor is under pressure to meet deadlines determined by fixed funding periods and passes this pressure on to the counterpart. The counterpart's slow pace of change may not simply be a result of reluctance or of cultural factors, but may be constrained

**¡SOMOS AMIGOS!**

One of the conclusions of an evaluation of Novib's gender and development policy in Peru and Colombia (*¡Somos Amigos!*, 1994) was that the promotion of South-South and in-country exchange and dialogue among counterparts (e.g. between women's organizations and mixed organizations) and among local gender experts and counterparts is an important strategy for promoting good gender practices.

It is also important to promote such an exchange when the debate around gender is constrained by emotionally charged stereotypes of 'those feminists' and 'those macho NGOs'. In the case of Peru and Colombia, both women's organizations and male-dominated mixed NGOs agreed that such images are largely out of date and that recent experiences of collaboration and exchange have proven that both parties have a lot to gain from concrete ways of cooperation, exchanging information, experiences and skills, and even result-oriented emulation, especially when mixed and women's organizations are working in similar fields, e.g. education, health, or the labour market. Addressing biases and stereotyping gives both types of organization new opportunities for strategic alliances and gender learning.

by limited resources, other funding deadlines it is expected to meet, changes in staffing, or other factors.

This raises the more general question of how well donors judge the timing and entry point of their interventions. Case study 2 (the farmers' union) illustrates problems arising from attempts to insert mechanisms for improving gender sensitivity into projects already under way, which had not taken account of women's needs and interests at the outset. Obviously donors should include gender considerations from the earliest stages of project planning, and indeed they should be woven into overall strategic planning at the level of country or regional programmes. But in many cases a donor agency may have already been involved with a particular counterpart for a long time when a new project is being put forward; if the ongoing relationship with the counterpart did not include a debate around gender from the start, it can be difficult and potentially conflictive to introduce it in midstream. Tact and openness in discussion are necessary to introduce gender issues into such relationships. However, this is not an argument for *not* introducing gender issues into ongoing partnerships. While case study 3 ('Pressing the claim...') is rightly critical of the limitations of the donor intervention, it also points out the positive effects of setting a new process in motion.

## Practising what we preach

And what about the organizational dynamics of both donor and counterpart? Several of the case studies reveal that not only is gender balance on the staff of the donor as important as that of the counterpart (but far less closely scrutinized by the donor), but that continuity of staff has a decisive effect on the continuity of attention to gender issues. People leave the organization or move to a different post; new and different people come in; the gender balance fluctuates, and so does the general level of gender sensitivity. The personalities of the individuals involved, their openness to change, and the degree to which they have appropriate skills, are also determinant in the success or failure of a gender intervention. Attention to gender awareness is necessary in the recruitment policies and procedures of the donor as well as the counterpart.

Yet, as the case studies above also reveal by omission, donor organizations usually show little or no interest in analysing their own roles and impacts; indeed, they seem to leave themselves out of the analysis altogether, to appear featureless, almost invisible. Their own internal debates and contradictions and the political and economic contexts in which they operate in their own countries remain hidden and undiscussed.

This brings us back, full circle, to the question of practising what we preach. A great deal of counterparts' resistance arises from their seeing that donor organizations are not changing their own practice in line with their gender policies. We often have higher expectations of counterpart organizations than we seem to require of our own, and we should be aware of, and work to overcome, these double standards. As donors, we need to reflect on our own organizations as well as our counterparts, to be aware of our assumptions, and to examine our own practice critically. Is it reasonable for us to expect from our counterparts what we do not practise ourselves?

Also, donors must be prepared to take on the criticisms of counterparts and to learn from them. Dialogue means that we have the right to question counterparts, but they also have the right to question us. Donor agencies that have listened to counterparts' criticism and changed their practice accordingly, particularly on gender, have found positive results in both North and South.

## Tools, knowledge, and skills

When the question of promoting greater gender equality in development cooperation with counterparts is raised, the response is often to demand tools by which this may be done (see for example case study 4 –'How far can we push?'). While this is a positive and practical response, this search for technical solutions – training, policy instruments, etc. – can also be seen as a retreat from the more emotionally demanding and less clear-cut questions of personal attitudinal change.

Further, there is a tendency to look for a standard model of intervention which can be applied across the board. If gender inequality exists in every country and every culture in the world, why is there no single strategy with which to address that inequality? What tools can we devise to do so? The simple fact is that there is no panacea. Each case is different, and there is no universally applicable recipe for success. Just as the problems – beyond the very general baseline of prevailing gender inequality – are specific to each case, so too are the solutions. The tools that can be used for any specific intervention, therefore, must be tailored to the situation being addressed.

Moreover, having acquired tools is no guarantee of a solution. In different hands, the same tool can be either constructive or destructive. The simple knife is a tool which can be used to support life, in the preparation of food; to save life, in surgery; or to kill. It can be used brutally and clumsily, or with infinite precision. Similarly, the tools used in development interventions – such as impact studies, evaluations, different kinds of training – can be used to good or bad effect, depending on the motivation for their use and the skill with which they are used. How those tools are used depends on factors such as the underlying values of the organization employing them, the knowledge, skills, and sensitivity of the people using them – and the political will to use them to the most beneficial effect.

In any case, before any tools can be employed, two prior conditions must be met, or must be built in the organization:

- the organization and its staff must have a culture of transparency and a mindset of openness and commitment to engaging with gender issues – that is, there must be readiness to change;
- the skills and capacity must be present in the organization to arrive at an understanding of the complexities of the organization, its situation in its external environment, and the stage it is at in its own organizational development, and from this understanding to analyse and diagnose the change needed and where the scope for change lies.

These two conditions – readiness to change and capacity to analyse the organization – correspond broadly with the first two stages of the 'roadmap' or framework for a process of gender and organizational change outlined below in chapter 6.

The choice of tools or technicques that can then be applied or devised depends very much on the nature of the change process that is diagnosed. The required change process may be at the level of putting gender on the agenda, of formulating a policy, of securing implementation of an existing policy, or of restructuring the organization. But it should also be recognized that the cry for tools reflects a rather static perception of gender inequality in development as a technical issue which can be addressed by means of technical solutions. It does not take sufficient account of the extent to which gender inequality is an emotional and psychological issue. Technical tools can be used to change behaviour and practice, but a longer, more transformative, more diffuse and therefore less easily measurable process is necessary to achieve the changes in individual attitude and organizational culture without which more equal gender relations are impossible.

## Note

1. For the concepts of practical and strategic gender needs, see Caroline Moser, 'Gender planning in the Third World: meeting practical and strategic gender needs', in Tina Wallace and Candida March (eds,), *Changing perceptions* (Oxford: Oxfam, 1991). The distinction between practical and strategic gender needs has been widely used in analyses of the outcomes of gender interventions. However this distinction is a problematic one, given its implicit assumption of a logical time sequence and of a hierarchical order of interests. A summary of policy approaches analysed in terms of their contribution to addressing women's practical and strategic needs in development cooperation may be found in Cecilia Andersen, 'Practical guidelines', in L. Ostergaard (ed.), *Gender and development: a practical guide* (London: Routledge, 1992), pp. 172-4.

implement gender policies (and to assimilate them, culturally and personally) faster than the donor agencies are themselves prepared to do. This is obviously unreasonable.

This question of timing brings into the foreground two concepts fundamental to the equal promotion of gender policies and good gender practice at home and abroad: transparency and accountability. These principles are as important within donor organizations as in the donor/counterpart relationship (for the latter, see Macdonald, 1994b: 10–11). In development NGDOs, both managers and staff undoubtedly see themselves, and their whole organization, as accountable in some sense to their counterparts, although this commitment may be qualified by the donor's superior economic power. Within their internal structures, however, particularly where the organization is hierarchically structured, people may well regard themselves as accountable only or principally to their superiors. The kind of accountability we are referring to here is broader: in terms of implementing gender policies and changing organizational culture and personal attitudes, managers are as accountable to their staffs as staff members are to managers, and men and women in the organization are equally mutually accountable. This mutual accountability, together with transparency and honesty in dialogue and decision-making, is part of the collective organizational learning and sharing of values involved in embedding gender at the heart of an organization.

### Constraints

There are a host of constraints to making organizations more gender-aware, and many of them are common to organizations in both the North and the South. Sara Longwe, in her article 'A development agency as a patriarchal cooking pot: the evaporation of policies for women's advancement'[1] gives a sharp and witty guide to the multitude of ways the gender status quo reasserts itself and resists any shift in the prevailing balance of power, both in development agencies in the North and in governmental and non-governmental institutions in the South. Longwe's account of how gender policy evaporates may be briefly summarized thus:

- procedures for verbal defence
  - denial – insist the problem doesn't exist
  - inversion – blame the victim
  - policy dilution – pretend existing policy is weaker than it actually is
- procedures for diversionary action
  - lip-service – admit to the problem, but do nothing
  - commission unnecessary or inappropriate research on the issue
  - shelve the research
- procedures for ineffectual organizational change
  - compartmentalization – set up a separate women's office or women's issues post on the periphery of decision-making structures
  - subversion – give the post to a person with no power or ability to achieve change
  - tokenism.

To these we could add:
- resistance disguised as incomprehension, where gender is simultaneously said to be a) too mystifying and complicated, and b) in need of 'a more refined and sophisticated analysis';
- resistance based on the idea that gender is a Northern, or 'Western', concept that we have no right to impose on Southern cultures, or (applied to gender in our own organizations) that it is a feminist obsession that distracts from the main issues: 'focusing on "male-dominated structures" is counterproductive'.

These arguments are also a kind of denial: the first, 'we don't understand what is meant by gender', is really a refusal to acknowledge the plain truth: a gender analysis says that relations between men and women are unequal, and this is unjust. The second begs the question: have *women* been asked whether this idea is foreign to their culture?

There are, however, institutional constraints on making firm links between gender issues with counterparts and gender issues at home. For instance, responsibility for internal policy in general is usually located institutionally in a different division or department from responsibility for external policy. This makes it hard to link strategies for achieving a more gender-fair practice inside the organization with strategies applied to work with overseas counterparts. It is also hard to develop coherent policy and practice on gender across different parts of the organization, which may well have different organizational cultures and histories. Moreover, just as bureaux concerned with gender and development in states and development administrations are often perched on the periphery of mainstream development concerns, as Anne Marie Goetz notes (1992: 7), so gender responsibles in NGDOs tend to be gender advisers and to have little or no decision-making powers, and gender units or focal points tend to be non-central and underresourced.

On the other hand, especially in smaller organizations, gender specialists, though usually located in a policy unit related to programmes and projects, tend to be called upon to assist or advise also on gender aspects of all other departments, including internal organizational development, personnel, education, campaigning, or lobbying, marketing, or to be expected to act as general 'watchdogs' on gender for the whole organization. So gender responsibles, as well as their specific brief of looking after gender issues in the programme work in the South, must keep an eye on the gender dimension of everything else as well, while other departments are allowed to neglect the development of their own gender expertise.

There are also constraints springing from personalities and personal attitudes. Particularly when gender is at issue, organizational and personal attitudes are almost impossible to disentangle: the personal *is* the political. For many gender activists, personal attitude and commitment is the bottom line – increasing the number of women in top management, for instance, will be useless if they are not the kind of women who will argue for gender equality. With regard to gender intervention with counterparts, several of the case studies above illustrate how a particular person's attitude towards gender issues can be decisive in either putting gender firmly on the agenda or sweeping it firmly off.

gender sensitivity without involving the political process of deep personal and institutional self-questioning, it is a meaningless exercise.

Tools are only useful when we know how to use them. They cannot be applied until the gender dynamics of the organization have been analysed, the problem areas diagnosed, and the specific kind of organizational change process necessary identified. As the Gender Route process (chapter 8) shows, the tools employed for change must be tailor-made to suit each organization and the specific change it wants to achieve. This is equally true for processes of change being promoted with counterpart organizations and processes of internal organizational change.

Moreover, the use of technical tools is necessary but not sufficient. As we have noted in chapter 3, technical solutions must be accompanied by culture and attitude change. What is needed is a process of *transformation*.

### Understanding of gender

Perhaps the most fundamental tool of all is a basic understanding of what 'gender' means. Yet the evidence from the interviews and some of the case studies in chapters 2 and 3 suggests that, outside of departments specifically concerned with gender, there still seems to be a generally imperfect understanding and internalization of information on what gender is about, even in agencies which claim good performance on gender. One observation made in an interview reveals a common misconception about gender: 'very few are familiar with the method, but it will be compulsory to know and use it in the future'. This response seems to rest on an understanding of 'gender' as merely a tool or method, not as an all-pervading system of power relations. Several interviewees stressed the lack of interest in gender among counterparts and highlighted the need to improve awareness of gender in project preparation or in country offices. Others pointed to the fact that 'gender very often ends up being only about women: [it is] necessary to broaden the debate'. But many people, particularly programme officers, themselves seem still to be thinking along WID lines, as if gender simply meant paying more attention to women as a target group. The basic idea that gender is about relations between men and women, especially power relations, still seems not entirely to have got through.

Admittedly, a lot of the available theoretical material is abstract and densely argued, and can be daunting to people with a high workload who need practical applications. It is the role of the change agent on gender to demystify and facilitate a process of gender learning on the basis of concrete and practical experiences. But it should also be recognized that it is the responsibility of everyone to analyse their work from a gender perspective and identify good gender practices, i.e. new and better ways of doing things.

### Tools, skills, and transformation

We have attempted to analyse why the integration of gender into our own organizational development seems so difficult and fraught with danger. For Northern donor organizations, some of the familiar strategies for dealing with gender with counterparts are also applicable to internal gender issues, principally those addressing behaviour, structures, and procedures in the organization. However, in both North and South, other strategies and forms of communication are clearly called for at the level of changing our own organizational culture.

This is the level at which transformation must take place if the organization is to be made truly gender-equal. No matter how radically or how often structures and procedures are changed, no matter what targets are set, if organizational culture is not changed, in the end nothing will really change. Change of this kind requires addressing a different – a deeper – level, because in order to achieve this transformation of personal attitudes and organizational culture, we are looking at psychological, rather than methodological changes. We need a solution that addresses the emotional problems associated with accepting gender equality, at the levels of both individual and organizational transformation. Arriving at such a solution requires triple-loop learning (chapter 1), a critical analysis of our organizational culture, collective questioning of the values underpinning our work, and commitment to behaviour and attitude change at the individual level; for, after all, an organization is just a purposeful association of individual people.

In this undertaking, perhaps what we should be crying out for is not tools but skills. Our analysis should come up first with a vision of the gender-sensitive organization to which we aspire and then with a series of strategies for making that vision a reality. But we also need skills specific to the kind of transforming processes we are envisaging here: skills in organizational analysis and diagnosis; skills in bringing people together, in promoting and facilitating dialogue, in creating a safe space within which these issues can be ventilated with the minimum of pain; skills in guiding institutional learning processes and collective strategizing; and skills in recording and socializing the learnings accomplished, to form a basis for the next cycle of learning. These may be new requirements for many development NGDOs, and we should be searching for ways to develop and nurture such skills.

### Increasing gender-awareness in organizations: some key factors

We conclude this chapter by outlining some of the factors identified as essential to the interlocking processes of organizational assessment and change involved in creating scope for gender-sensitive organizational development in any organization, either in the North or the South.[2]

- *Commitment to gender equality and the promotion of gender sensitivity.* This is the first prerequisite for any process of change leading to more gender-sensitive organizational development. Ultimately, if the change is to be meaningful and is to carry institutional weight, this commitment must reach up to the highest levels in the organization's management.

- *Understanding and analysis.* The next requirement is to unpack the external historical, political, economic, social and cultural context in which gender

interventions are being made; the history and culture of the organization itself and of gender within it, and the priorities and power of men and women in the organization:
- analyse the roles of stakeholders, both men and women;
- remember that changes in the external environment, 'macro' organizational changes (changes in political direction, restructuring, new director), and changes in staff all impact on an organization's capacity to work effectively on gender, either temporarily or in the longer term;
- be aware of the differences in implementing gender policies in Asia, Africa, Latin America – and Europe. But be aware of the common ground, too – and learn from it;
- recognize the other factors which may be at play besides gender;
- gender-disaggregated research is essential, as is training to improve everyone's competence in developing a gender analysis and internalizing knowledge about gender issues.

- *Listening and sensitivity*. It is important to start where an organization is at:
  - listen to the views of both men and women. Be aware of gender discussions going on in the organization;
  - consider the cultural specificities (both external and organizational);
  - are the conditions present (e.g. in terms of the number of women involved) for significant and lasting change?;
  - be aware of the difference between change at the organizational level and at the personal level, and of the different expectations involved;
  - avoid imposing views and attitudes, e.g. by supporting links between Southern counterparts and other organizations, supporting Southern feminist organizations, networking and exchanges of different kinds.

- *Legitimizing the debate on gender*. This includes making gender awareness a strategic objective in the organization, training all staff, and ensuring adequate resources for gender work. Build on any existing debates on gender in the organization. Gender should not have to compete with other areas of concern for the organization (e.g. poverty, race, class); on the contrary, the organic relationship of gender with all these issues needs to be fully recognized in policy and practice.

- *Being aware of our own power*. In general, people who are powerful in an organization, either through their position or their personal qualities, need to analyse their power. More specifically, in the donor/counterpart relationship, donor organizations need to recognize and analyse the difficulty and dilemmas of being donors. Project funding should not be made conditional upon change in the counterpart. However, donors should not be afraid of setting minimum standards and making demands on the basis ofthem. But this entails the responsibility for donors of 'practising what they preach'.

- *Dialogue, not confrontation, as the motor of change.* Dialogue aims to explore the positions of all stakeholders; to create consensus; to understand resistance and the reasons for it:
  - dialogue needs time to develop and mature, along with appropriate support during the process;
  - dialogue costs money;
  - true dialogue requires transparency, sharing of experiences, readiness to learn from each other, avoidance of alienating or mystifying language;
  - counterparts should also be encouraged to assess donor practices from a gender perspective.

- *Transparency of communication.* Transparent and honest dialogue on the organization's internal gender dynamics is vitally important within all organizations, between all levels and departments. Between donors and counterparts, donors should have a clear statement of their own policy and values, and should be honest about how successfully they have met their own goals in implementing a gender policy. Southern counterparts should feel able to be clear about their own constaints, as well as being able to challenge Northern double standards. Donors should also be clear and specific about the objectives of the gender interventions they promote and the results they expect.

- *Achieving attitude change.* Formal and structural changes to an organization, such as arriving at gender parity, are important but not sufficient. Organizations consist of individuals, and the power balance needs to be changed at both the personal and the institutional level. But change that may strike at deep beliefs and strong emotions is never easy or automatic. Men's (and sometimes women's) fear of the far-reaching change gender equality implies is very real: we need to stress positive aspects and the benefits to all of gender fairness, and to avoid coercive argument.

- *Change agents.* The agent of change needs to be both modest (because the task is large and difficult) and ambitious (because the goal is worth fighting for). Consider using local consultants to facilitate attitude change.

- *Men and women.* The gender debate should include an exploration of male/female differences (e.g. in organizational and management styles), without disempowering either side. There should be room for a culture of mutual respect. At the same time, this should not preclude the discussion of patriarchy in society at large as the main obstacle to gender equity, and in particular its impact on the culture and functioning of our own organizations. Issues of masculinity should be included in gender training.

- *Alliance building.* Strategic alliances need to be built with both men and women, donors and counterparts, across departments, institutions, regions. Informal consultations help to build alliances, whether with directors or with women in counterpart organizations.

- *Resourcing.* Real support for dialogue and change requires real resources, and the budget is most often the point at which the rhetoric of equality is put to the test. Are donors prepared to commit sufficient funds and support for a long-term change process in counterpart organizations? And in their own?

- *Patience, realism, flexibility.* Work on gender is a long and sometimes painful process. We should not have unrealistic expectations of how rapidly change can be achieved. We need to be aware of the added burden on women in the organization entailed by serious gender work; and of the added burden on the organization in terms of monitoring, reporting, developing skills, etc. We must be able to be patient, to accept failure and doubt and to keep on questioning ourselves. And donors should not expect counterpart organizations to develop gender sensitivity more rapidly than donors themselves.

- *Learning and creativity.* Creating scope for gender sensitivity is a collective learning process that requires a creative approach:
  - a participative, action-learning process is a prerequisite for promoting gender sensitivity;
  - make creative use of existing structures and customs, and learn from the ways local people use them;
  - use different diversity issues to nourish debate: diversity can provide a fresh entry point for overcoming blockages and resistance.

- *Indicators.* For both quantitative and qualitative change, indicators need to be agreed by all parties from the outset, based on a common understanding of what gender equality means in practice. Similarly, the objectives, expectations (anticipated results) and 'bottom lines' of all parties need to be clearly specified and mutually agreed at the start of any gender intervention.

## Notes

1. In M. Macdonald, ed., *Women's rights and development: vision and strategy for the twenty-first century*, Oxfam Discussion Paper 6. Oxford: Oxfam 1995.

2. This is a compilation of the list of observations and recommendations applying to work on both fronts – work with counterparts and work within donor agencies – which emerged from discussions at the 1995 *Eurostep* gender workshop.

# 5 Imagining a gender-sensitive organization

What would a gender-sensitive organization look like? It is easy enough to describe a gender-blind organization: we are surrounded by them. There is probably no government institution, company, church, university, trade union, or NG(D)O on earth that practises total gender equality. While we acknowledge that the ideal cannot be met in the short term, we can try to imagine what the features of a more gender-sensitive organization would be and to arrive at an idea of what qualitative change can be brought about by gender-aware organizational development. This chapter looks at some of the key aspects of an organization that potentially determine its gender sensitivity or gender equality:

- the 'shape' of the organization in terms of the distribution of decision-making power;
- the balance of women and men on the staff, and particularly in management and policy- or decision-making roles;
- organizational culture and style;
- the day-to-day functioning of the organization – is it woman-friendly, or even people-friendly?

## Organizational shape: flat or peaked?

What is the relationship between the formal structures of power and decision-making in an organization and its gender equality or gender sensitivity? In two papers on gender and organizations, Anne Marie Goetz (1992: 12; 1995: 8) examines the questions of whether hierarchical, bureaucratic organizational structures are necessarily antithetical to gender sensitivity in organizational environments and to feminist outcomes, and, conversely, whether feminist organizations are intrinsically more participatory and inclusive and based on more consensual decision-making. There is a wide range of opinion among theorists on how essentially or inherently masculine or feminine these forms are. What is clear is that hierarchies in every aspect of life, not excluding development NG(D)Os, usually have a preponderance of men at the top. In this sense hierarchies are male *in practice*, although it cannot be claimed beyond argument that the hierarchical structure itself is male *in essence*.

Moreover, there is no conclusive evidence that abolishing hierarchy as an organizational form will solve the problem of male dominance of organizations. Goetz concludes that the flat organization is not necessarily woman-friendly in either culture or structure. 'Collective and consensual management does not eradicate problems of domination' (Goetz 1992: 12); there are other ways of establishing and maintaining dominance. Flat, decentralized organizational structures may actually even contribute to making gender issues invisible, because of the amount of energy and time consumed in collective decision-making and the high level of insecurity attendant on these organizational forms (ibid.).

Caroline Moser (1993: 138) raises an even greater challenge. She points out that, in practice, the non-hierarchical structures to which many feminist women's organizations have been committed have not on the whole been strong enough to operate effectively beyond a very limited sphere of influence, and have remained outside the mainstream, not understood or taken seriously by bureaucracies. Feminist principles of self-realization, equality, anti-elitism, and 'sisterhood' have encouraged the formation of structureless groups with flexible, reactive agendas. While these have provided non-competitive, supportive environments conducive to confidence building and equal participation and diametrically opposed to the bureaucratic model, Moser writes:

> *To date, the non-hierarchical structures of feminist institutions have made few inroads into existing structures, nor sufficiently proved their professional competence to deliver and implement in practice.*

The experience of *Eurostep* member agencies neither confirms nor denies these conclusions. Some have found that in the process of restructuring and scaling-up their organizations have become both more hierarchical – with men rising to the top of the pyramid – and less woman-friendly. On the other hand, the presence of a hierarchical structure dominated by men has not *per se* prevented organizations like Oxfam, Novib, or Hivos from becoming increasingly gender-sensitive.

Thus it appears that there is not a necessary correlation between alternative organizational forms and women-friendly outcomes and attitudes. Organizational structure is just one of an ensemble of interrelated factors which can either encourage or hinder the acceptance and adoption of gender issues. Moser (1993: 138) concludes that 'the degree to which women's organizations and hierarchies can coexist is not proven. At the end of the day, some level of hierarchy, with accountability and effectiveness, is necessary.' However, if an organization is going to have any degree of hierarchy in its makeup, space and mechanisms for bottom–up flows of information, consultation, and decision-making from lower levels *must,* eventually, be formally built into its structure. This is a question of organizational *democracy.* In Nicaragua, for instance, the most democratic organizations are also the most gender-sensitive. It should be noted, however, that the term 'democracy' is being used here in a fundamentalist sense as participative rather than representative democracy, requiring the widest possible participation of both women and men on equal terms.

### Gender parity: is it enough?

Achieving a critical mass of women in organizations is considered by many experts to be a necessary and priority goal in attaining gender equality. They argue that by virtue of being present women inevitably bring new and different perspectives and become catalysts for change.[1]

## TOKENISM

Tokenism occurs when an organization in which the dominant groups (white people, men) are overwhelmingly represented tries to deflect criticism of its insensitivity to gender, colour, disability, etc., by recruiting a single individual or a very small minority from the group at issue. A token may be the first or only ethnic minority person in a white organization, the first or only woman in an all-male organization, etc. Tokenism tends to produce two interlocking effects.

*Disempowerment by the spotlight.* The token is highly visible; everyone knows what she does. She has little privacy. Anyone else can disappear into the anonymity of the group but the token cannot. This places enormous pressure on the way she functions, partly because the token is held responsible for the future of the other members of her group in the organization: if she does badly she will make it harder for other members of her group to get into the organization or to succeed in it. There are three typical responses to the spotlight pattern:
- becoming a 'super' example of the majority ('Mrs Thatcher'; 'one of the boys');
- becoming invisible (the syndrome of the 'frozen rabbit', who does nothing at all so as not to be seen);
- adopting a radical stance: pinned down in her exceptional position, the token manifests herself as being more radical than she would normally be within her own group of like-minded people.

*Majority group cohesion.* The presence of a token causes the majority to react more strongly as a group, whether intentionally or unintentionally. The difference between the members of the majority group seem to be erased or reduced by language use, jokes, codes, common experiences. Men start to behave in a more 'male' fashion if a woman joins their department. This makes it extremely difficult for the token woman to join in, with the result that she becomes isolated. She is faced with the difficult choice between adapting and joining in, starting from a position of considerable disadvantage and having to abandon or compromise many of her own values in order to be accepted, or being excluded. (Adapted from De Beuk, 1995: nos 3 and 32)

A critical mass (in numerical terms) of women present in an organization, not only in management but also at lower levels, should at least draw attention to a number of practical women's needs and interests, such as childcare provision and flexible working hours. There is considerable research (see Goetz 1992: 13) to show that women policy-makers in different national contexts have consistently articulated women's interests on issues such as childcare, maternity benefits, and equal pay, and have tended to have

## The people-friendly organization

The foregoing section has touched on the tension that often exists between organizational goals and the life goals of people working in the organization. In traditional, male-dominated organizations, what workers do when they are not at work – even what they *are* besides being workers – is of no relevance. On the whole, this has mattered much less for men, because their domestic, family lives have been overwhelmingly taken care of by women. Historically, women's responsibility for the home and children has been a subsidy which enables men to spend long hours at work, to travel at short notice, and to carry on their working lives without any irruption of the private into the public arena.

Just as women's domestic labour has made it possible for men to behave at work as though they have no private lives, so the corresponding identification of women with the private, domestic sphere is used to disqualify women from full participation in waged work. Women's sexuality and reproductive functions are seen as disruptive of ongoing work and the pursuit of organizational goals (see Acker, 1992: 255). Women cannot escape their private lives; men are not allowed to have them.

This arrangement is bad for everybody; but changing the situation means changing, not the people, but the organization. Reproduction and sexuality may indeed disrupt ongoing work, but only in the currently prevalent male-defined structures, and according to a male-defined notion of disruption; they may be incompatible with the orderly and rational pursuit of organizational goals, but only if these have been defined in a way which takes no account of the nature of the human resources necessary to pursue them.

A people-friendly organization, then, will be aware of people's lives outside the work situation. It will take account of women's reproductive roles and functions and plan them into its structure, work methodologies, strategic planning, administration, and physical arrangements, instead of merely grafting gender onto an existing structure. It will recognize that both women and men are parents, partners, family members, and workers, and have both private and public lives – and that what happens in their private lives impacts upon their performance as workers and can both enrich or impoverish it. It will therefore enable men as well as women to carry out either reproductive and caring responsibilities in the home and the community, for instance by providing flexible working hours and leave arrangements. It will develop an organizational culture which is sympathetic to people's having a life outside the office, allowing people to have feelings and devoting organizational space to discussion of personal matters. Furthermore, it will recognize people's diverse sexual preferences and family/living arrangements.

Introducing or enhancing these values in an organization certainly requires flexibility, adaptability, and assigning value to informal ways of exchanging information, making opinions heard, and taking decisions. Often these can be more effective and responsive to actual needs in the organization than the more rigid formal channels and procedures. But this is not an argument for the abandonment of all forms of structure, system, or regulation. A balance has to be struck between this kind of flexibility and human responsiveness in the organization, and the equally important values of efficiency and cost-effectiveness.

---

## WHAT MAKES AN ORGANIZATION WOMAN-FRIENDLY?

Indicators for measuring the woman-friendliness of an organization are highly contextual and culturally specific. However, the following indicators could be considered as a general guide:

- materials displayed in the building, e.g. pictures, posters and other graphic material, announcements of meetings and activities, are not disrespectful of women;
- appropriate facilities, such as lavatories, childcare, transport are provided;
- there are procedures to deal with sexual harassment;
- men and women do not make nasty jokes or comments about the other sex;
- diversity of styles between men and women is viewed as a strength of the organization;
- provision of working arrangements which enable the combination of work with reproductive/caring responsibilities outside the workplace, such as part-time employment, flexible working hours and leave arrangements, etc.

---

### Conclusion

In the end, whatever structures are chosen and behaviour change promoted, there is 'no substitute for the injection of an *explicit* concern with gender equity, and the exercise of leadership or vision in women's interests' (Goetz 1995: 6). This may be aided by the presence of more women staff, but not guaranteed. In the long term, a more thorough-going transformation of the organization's structure, systems, and culture is called for. Some form of affirmative action programme is a fundamental starting point.

So, what *would* a gender-sensitive organization look like? Although every organization must find its own model of gender sensitivity, we can sum up by listing some very general features that would seem essential to making any organization more gender-sensitive and more gender-equal.[4]

- Gender equality should be a priority not only in the organization's mission statement, general objectives, and policies, but in its internal regulations (recruitment procedures, terms and conditions for workers, etc.).

- Adequate resources should be devoted to putting such policies into practice.

# Gender and organizational change: a roadmap

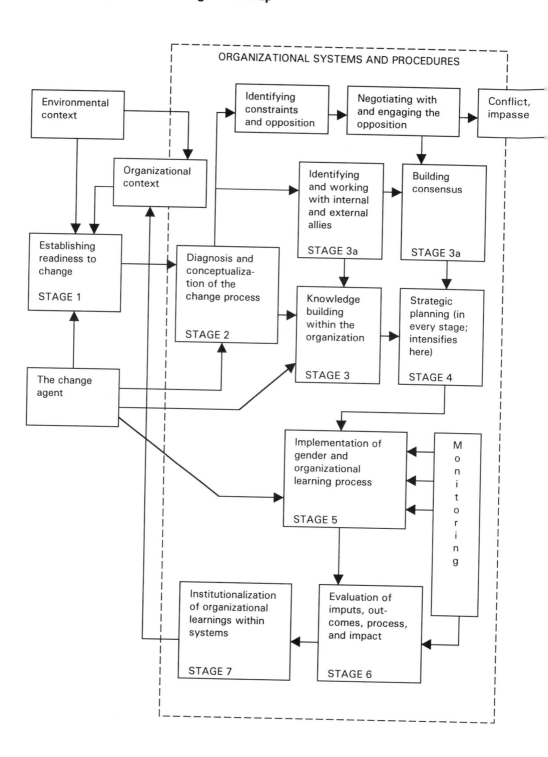

## Stages in the process of change

*Stage 1: Assessing/establishing readiness to change*
How can we judge when an organization is ready for change? Readiness for change seems to be a combination of political willingness to change, aided by a climate of transparency in the organization, and 'ripeness', detectable perhaps at moments when the organization becomes *uneasy* about a given issue. Moments of unease often coincide with moments of change such as the appointment of a new director or a new funding period, or, externally, a change in government or new legislation affecting development cooperation or social policy (which could affect women's rights and entitlements, labour law, etc.). Strategic planning often offers a chance to evaluate and assess readiness to change, as do project evaluation exercises.

These moments of unease, of faltering poise, can create space for change to occur – although a prerequisite, as we have remarked in chapter 1, is the will to change. However, a perception of ripeness is clearly not in itself a sufficient starting point. The first step in assessing whether the organization is ready to change is to analyse its present situation. How do we know 'where the organization is at'? This can be determined principally by looking at two things: the organization's external, environmental context and its internal, organizational context. From these emerge conditions which pressure the organization toward change, while the organization's leadership and key change agents and constituencies within provide and build commitment to the change intervention.

1. The *environmental* context of an organization is the external world in which it is situated: the international, national, cultural, political and economic context in which it operates. How does this environment affect the organization? What are the push and pull factors that may either drive it towards change or hold it back? Some factors that should be examined follow.

- Look at the broad national context in which the organization is working. Is it favourable to the work of NG(D)Os or not? What official help does the government give to these organizations, and what constraints does it place upon them? Has this changed recently, and in what direction? (For example, in a new NGO act passed recently in Kenya, the government ruled that all organizations had to be registered.) If the government decides it is opposed to promoting gender, you are much more constrained in the changes you can attempt to make, because the political and social environment is not conducive to what you want to do. So you also need to look at the following points.

- What is the legal system and the political situation under which the organization is working? How does this affect organizational stability, and how much room for manoeuvre is there?

- Draw up a social map of the country of operation, including a list of organizations working in it. What reference points will the organization have in, say, a country just emerging from war? It may be working closely with international emergency/relief organizations, which tend to be notorious for their machismo. Map what other organizations are doing, and also the history of organizing/activism in the country.

- Look at relevant international phenomena. Most international economic developments over the past decade – neoliberal market economics, structural adjustment, generalized political conservatism – are bad news for women. What constraints does this imply for the organization? Is it moving forward, or retrenching?

- Many organizations are made up of people from different cultural values or backgrounds. This cultural context is part of the environmental context, and can influence an organization's readiness to change. Analyse the implications of 'cultural' values (e.g. dominant or accepted ways of organization) for acceptance of the particular gender effort being proposed. Are there conflicts in communication in the organization deriving from, or related to, these differences?

2. The internal *organizational* context includes the organization's history, principles, ideological basis, structure, etc., and how they have developed. What are the elements in an organization (e.g. leadership) and the aspects of its health (e.g. instability, strains, processes of expansion and contraction) that affect its readiness to change? Look at:
- the history and background of the organization;
- its ideology: what assumptions will influence the gender analysis of the organization (and therefore the diagnosis of what kind or level of change is needed)?
- mandates;
- values;
- resources: is the organization financially stable? Are there available resources to enable the organization to innovate?
- management style;
- kind of leadership: is the leadership committed to the change or to a particular vision to be achieved?
- moments of change or flux, e.g. change of director, from a man to a woman (both a cause and a factor);
- a felt need within the organization that change is necessary because of internal strains (e.g. increasing bureaucratization) leading to reduced effectiveness;
- poor achievement of goals;
- need for greater accountability to primary stakeholders.

3. In particular, the *donor/counterpart relationship* involves two different environmental and organizational contexts and the interplay between them, which can be productive or obstructive. This also applies to Southern NGOs (which may themselves be the counterparts of Northern donors) in their relationship with their target or beneficiary groups.

- Donors need to evaluate at level of the organization itself, not just at the level of counterpart projects; if an evaluation of projects reveals problems, the donor needs to look at itself as well as the counterparts and their projects.

- What is the influence of counterparts in generating readiness to change? Counterparts are part of the environmental context of a donor (as donors are of the counterpart), but the way donors and counterparts relate is part of their own organizational context: on both sides, some are resistant on gender, others in favour. Managers can use these attitudes to buttress their arguments for or against change.

- The learnings and demands of counterparts can push donors towards change, if they are open to it. On the other hand, donors are often powerful enough to ignore counterpart demands if they wish, and if there is no pressure (internal or external) to get them to listen.

- At the same time, with change efforts directed at counterparts, it is the role of the donor to introduce ideas for change, establish dialogue, and so on. This is not to suggest that the counterpart, or some people in the counterpart, never has its own ideas for change. Often, the most important thing a donor can do is to support an existing pressure for change within the counterpart organization.

- The flipside is that donors are part of the environmental context of counterparts! Often when donors look at counterparts they leave themselves out of the picture of the counterpart and its environment. They need to look at the role of *all* donors, not just themselves, in the external context of the counterpart.

*The characteristics of the change agent* and the *culture of the organization* also influence readiness for change. These will be dealt with in more detail in the next chapter.

Any or all of these factors can contribute to an organization's readiness or reluctance to change. For instance, a national development administration's background in a highly militarized colonial service may leave a legacy in the current gender balance of its staff, or in a militaristic or adventurist kind of workstyle, but the organization may also survive in a difficulty by being flexible and open to change (see Goetz 1992: 11). Or an NGO which has sprung from a tradition of popular struggle or national liberation may present ideological obstacles and be rigid about dismantling them. Significant increases or decreases in funding, or an organizational history of insecure or fluctuating funding, can have a severe effect on the presence and power of women on the staff.

Readiness to change may be very limited: sometimes an organization (i.e. probably its senior management) will accept gender training only. Even if the process does not at this point go on to subsequent stages along the lines of this framework, this information can be useful, for instance in understanding why others in the organization act as they do. This can help later in dealing with resistance to change.

## Stage 2: Diagnosis and conceptualization of the change process

The conceptualization stage is an opportunity to increase acceptance of the idea of change, pushing back the boundaries of what people are ready for. The change agent will probably play a role here, together with opinion leaders in the organization, in helping to identify the problem.

This is the basic diagnostic stage. Once you have arrived at a set of understandings about the state of the organization, you need to build a hypothesis about the process of change, based on that analysis. What kind of change, at what level, is necessary? Does the change need to be at the level of behaviour (either personal or collective), structures, or basic principles?

This raises the prior question (which your analysis of the state of the organization should have pointed to, if not delineated in detail): what is the problem? This is the starting point for the process, and should be based on your organizational analysis. It is also the point at which expectations of the result of change might be expressed. How could change take place?

There will probably be competing interests in the organization, who will raise the question, What makes you think that gender is the problem, not something else? This is the stage at which you will have to justify diagnosing the problem as gender-based. Or you may have to admit that it isn't. Gender isn't always the problem! Other changes in the organization (e.g. 'downsizing', restructuring) may be bringing about unwelcome changes in its gender dynamics, but these will probably be more usefully addressed at the more general level, not just by addressing the gender aspects.

## Stage 3: Building knowledge and consensus within the organization

Building on the basic identification of the problem and the kind of change necessary in broad terms, which you have established in stage 2, a more refined and detailed process of diagnosis of particular parts of the organization where change could take place can be undertaken. This involves wide-ranging consultation, aimed at getting people throughout the organization to articulate what they see as the problem and broadening the base of 'ownership' of the diagnosis of the problem.

This consultation is one of the most basic elements of organizational learning, leading to shared ownership of the diagnosis. People need to feel that they are part of a process; the more people in an organization you get to define what they see as the problem, the broader and more inclusive a picture you get. Therefore, talk to as many people in the organization, in as many different departments and at as many different levels, as possible.

Different groups in the organization (workers, managers, women, men, etc.) will define the problem differently or will identify different problems. In this way, you build up knowledge about the problem or problems in the organization and about the people involved, via their perceptions of the problems.

It is important, too, that this information be widely shared: it is not enough for the change agent to gather information about people's perceptions of a problem and their positions on it. Another way of arriving at and sharing a diagnosis is a process of self-diagnosis carried out by a group of colleagues and facilitated by a relative outsider, in which the participants come up with their own analysis and identify the challenges for the organization.

*Stage 3a: Identifying and working with internal and external allies.* The process of problem diagnosis may generate lots of defensiveness, but also lots of thinking and lots of *silence*. People are challenged, they are suddenly faced openly with the fact that there are differences of opinion – maybe very large ones – among their colleagues; uncomfortable issues which have been suppressed or glossed over for some time may threaten to come into the open. What is not talked about may be as important a part of the diagnosis as what is.

The change agent(s) will thus need to find people inside the organization (and outside it, if appropriate or necessary – they will give a different perspective altogether), with whom to work on building consensus around the problem. People external to the organization could be friendly consultants or trainers – but they need to be people who know your organization well. These internal and external allies will be different according to the nature and structure of the organization. You could build alliances with women at the lower end of the organization, or with sympathetic senior managers if they exist, or with women going through a similar process in another organization. The particular issues will be different in different organizations, for instance between an organization where women are in the majority and one where they are not, or between a 'flat' organization and a relatively hierarchical one.

This stage also involves identifying *constraints and opposition.* These include resources (time, financial, human) and money, and also the specific location of decision-making power in the organization. It also involves identifying not only allies but opponents, and finding out why they are opposed to the idea of change. A rounded picture of everyone's interests is being built up throughout this stage.

Again, this is not a linear process but is likely to involve revisiting issues and looking at them several times from many different points of view, which will entail an ongoing redefinition of the problem and a refinement of the diagnosis. In fact, probably none of these stages will have a clearly defined 'beginning' and 'end'. For instance, assessing readiness to change and identifying the kind of change necessary (and possible), are closely interlocking tasks: an organization may be ready for one kind of change but not another; it may be ready to address one issue but extremely resistant to addressing another. The processes of knowledge building and consensus building may well still be going on, or may have moved into new phases, even while implementation is under way.

*Stage 3b: Building consensus around the issue.* Building consensus around the issue identified is arguably half the battle of achieving change. This whole process is very interactive and ongoing – a kind of 'political knitting'.[4] In fact, we are doing it every time we raise a gender issue with colleagues or managers, on a daily basis. Consensus-building inevitably involves having the same discussions over and over, proceeding by very small steps. It requires a lot of patience and persistence. Renegotiation of the issues being addressed and of the process is in this sense ongoing, so a flexible approach to the planning and implementation of the change process is vital to build ownership of the entire process.

Some participants at the workshop drew attention to opposite processes: dealing with resistance, and *confrontation* as well as consensus-building, especially the problem of conflict between top management and the gender team or other change agents. This stage could therefore also involve the analysis and resolution of conflicts. To win over managers, it is necessary to understand their interests and negotiate on the basis of this understanding, searching for the arguments that will speak to those interests while not eroding gender interests.

Clearly, consensus is preferable, but not always possible. One participant described the experience of working in a mixed organization right through to the final stage of institutionalization of learnings, without ever having achieved consensus on gender as an issue. However, the experience showed that in such a case gender would not be taken on right at the heart of the organization. Particularly if there are no allies in management, it is hard to get from stage 4 (strategic planning) to stage 5 (implementation); the process is less clean and clear, and is full of emotion. But this should not be a reason for giving up: you have to deal with the organization you are in.

We probably have to recognize that in some organizations internal consensus may never be achievable. You may effect slight change, with help from external allies, but you probably will not get gender *organically integrated*. Here the risk is that you may end up with a tension between gender and all other aspects of the organization. It will probably have to be admitted, in such cases, that the organization was not yet ready for change on gender issues.

### Stage 4: Strategic planning

One of the key characteristics of gender and organizational change interventions is the clear link made between the strategic objectives of the organization and the intervention. For this linkage to propel the change process fruitfully, managers who shape organizational mandates, staff whose actions translate those mandates into action on the ground, the change agents themselves, and, ideally, the organization's clients must negotiate (or renegotiate) the meanings that underlie those objectives. In doing so, they will open up spaces for reinterpretation and extension of the boundaries of those meanings in ways that are contextually appropriate and 'do-able'. The strategic planning stage encompasses this renegotiation of meanings and the arrival at some basic agreement over the direction, depth, boundaries, and starting place of the change intervention.

The strategic planning stage builds further on the previous stages. It breaks down the desired overall change into specific objectives to which people can relate in terms of their own work responsibilities. The strategic plan will detail and specify different objectives for different layers and departments of the organization, while clarifying how these relate to one another in terms of the overall change to be achieved. A strategic planning exercise ideally draws in all participants and clarifies each one's particular responsibility and task within the overall change process.

Once the objectives are clarified, they are then operationalized in an action plan or operational plan, which outlines the activities to be undertaken, the inputs required in terms of resource allocation (financial, material, human), the expected and desired results and outputs, and a timeline.

It is worth emphasizing that strategic planning includes decision-making around allocation of resources: whatever the readiness to change of the organization and its managers, top management must be convinced of the need to devote the resources necessary to carry out the change process.

### Stage 5: Implementation of the gender and organizational learning process

The critical point here is that the implementation stage must be a flexible process of action-learning, whereby the participants begin to feel responsible for – to 'own' – the change process. Starting places are more often at the periphery than at the core, in the field rather than at the centre. It is important to work with teams of people who normally work together so that the innovations arising from practice can be integrated quickly into standard operating procedures, problems can be addressed immediately, and practice modified appropriately. It is important also to move quickly from training to a focus on work practices and to the involvement of larger and larger circles of decision-making within the organization. In some contexts, the involvement of insiders in broader networks of outside expertise and solidarity may further legitimize and inform the change process within the organization.

The implementation of action plans should be facilitated by experienced trainer–facilitators, with organizational and gender-sensitizing skills, who are accepted and respected by the counterpart organization or the staff of the organization. The trainer–facilitators should ideally be supervised by a core group of experienced gender and organizational development experts – these will normally be the gender team of the organization, if it has one. This is a collective action-learning process carried out by the organization, and should ideally involve everyone in it. Novib's Gender Route (see the box in chapter 8) is an example of such an action-learning process.

### Stage 6: Evaluation of inputs, outcomes, process and impact

Typically, the evaluation of a process of organizational change that seeks to improve the gender sensitivity and gender equality of an organization would look at:

- the outcomes and impacts of a gender programme on the knowledge and skills of staff, organizational quality, and programme quality;
- the causal factors that have led to change or lack of it;
- the strengths and weaknesses in the programme's process;
- the changes that need to be made to the gender programme in subsequent phases.

Some areas in which an evaluation might look at the impacts of a process of organizational change around gender include the following:
- Knowledge and skills of staff
  - increased understanding of gender and of the link between gender, programme quality and organizational change;
  - acquisition of action-learning skills, include an ability to influence others;
  - improved training and facilitation skills for gender team and trainers.
- Organizational quality
  - new, more gender-fair policies;
  - improvements in operating systems;
  - improved information flows between levels of the system;
  - more efficient use of time;
  - better working relationships between male and female colleagues;
  - changes in the attitudes of male staff towards female colleagues.
- Programme quality
  - improvements in women's access to and control over resources;
  - enhancement of women's knowledge and ability to organize for their rights;
  - improved health, security, mobility for women;
  - systematization of such changes ('one swallow doesn't make a summer').[5]

Information on these aspects can be gathered using open-ended questionnaires followed up by discussions between gender responsibles, other members of staff, and researchers or consultants. This information enables evaluators to establish the impacts and outcomes of the gender programme on different people in the organization, to classify these as they relate to changes in knowledge, attitude or behaviour, and to measure the relative degree of change achieved.

*Stage 7: Institutionalization of the organization's learnings*
This institutionalization of learnings is the real point at which gender sensitivity is moved from the periphery of the organization to its very heart, and work around promoting gender equality throughout the organization is no longer just a 'fringe' activity carried out by a group of enthusiasts. If clear learnings emerge from the process, if systems change, if there are changes in the ways people work and live together, these need to be institutionalized. An important part of this process is training and discussion with senior managers on the gender and organizational development processes and their outcomes and impacts. Thus the process of change is linked to institutional outcomes, and better practice is more firmly ensured.

However, it is wise not to save this whole stage to the very end. Information should be being fed through to senior managers throughout the process, to prepare them and keep them in touch with the process. This helps them too to own the process of change.

Finally, the learnings become part of the organizational context, completing the cycle. You can tell that this has happened when *all managers* take account of gender routinely and regularly. This is the gauge of successful institutionalization of the learnings.

## Points for discussion

*Understanding and owning processes of change*

Two key constraints frequently brought up in discussions about changing organizational policy and practice on gender are, first, people's difficulty with understanding change processes and, second, their resistance to accepting them. There is no denying that changing gender relations in an organization is a highly emotional, as well as a highly political, project. Exploring organizational culture in detail can touch on very personal issues and sensitive issues of power – not just structures of power but questions of how individuals wield power, questions of one's own use of power. Difficulties may arise in judging readiness to change and in judging whether to promote such readiness subtly by means of alliance building and networking inside and outside the organization.

In all regions of the world, when organizations go through processes of change, they almost always come up against gender as a central challenge. Gender becomes an issue in all other areas of institutional change. But what is the specific difficulty of achieving change with respect to gender? We see that the failure to change certain things (particularly as regards gender relations in the organization) over many years and after many initiatives of various kinds shows us that we have to find out how organizations learn and how they *resist* learning – how they can reproduce the dominant model of gender relations in the very process of learning. How, for instance, can we dialogue with men on gender equality in language they understand and accept, without being coopted into the discourse of the powerful and silencing the women's voice once again? This vicious circle has to be broken, perhaps by going back yet one more stage and looking critically at how dialogue is carried on in organizations, between women and men, between more and less powerful actors. The more truly democratic and equal the dialogue is, the more people will feel able to own concepts that may be new to them and the process of change.

There are many skills women can – and ultimately must – acquire to be able to work effectively within basically male organizations, or organizations which resist recognizing their own gendered structures and culture: skills in communication and listening; skills in understanding how information is produced, circulated, and controlled in organizations; skills in negotiation, conflict resolution, problem analysis, decision-making, assertiveness, leadership. Yet very few gender experts have experience or training in management and organizational development in the traditional sense – probably fewer, these days, than the number of managers of either sex who have experienced some kind of gender training. This means we may not have tools to address the problem which will necessarily be understood or accepted by those who are part of the problem. Disagreement between gender teams and senior managers is not always the 'fault' of management, uncomfortable as this realization is. We seem to be speaking a different language from others (principally men) in the organization when it comes to talking about gender.

There thus appears to be a great need for gender experts and organizational development experts to exchange knowledge, insights, and skills: understanding organizational change is helpful if we are to become more effective as regards gender, and, conversely, understanding the dynamics of gender relations can contribute much to an understanding of organizational change.

### Involving men in the change process

One of the major advantages of a gender rather than a WID approach in development interventions[6] is that it brings men back into the picture and reminds us that good development for women cannot be achieved without looking at the interrelation between men's and women's relative roles, responsibilities, and power. Conceptualizing the issues in terms of gender relations rather than 'women's role' has redirected attention towards men's role and men's gender interests. At the same time, globalizing economic trends worldwide, resulting in rising male unemployment and a corresponding rise in female employment (albeit on far less favourable terms), mean that all over the world, women are increasingly becoming the main, or only, providers of family income; and this has seriously jolted the traditional assumptions linking masculinity with a man's ability to be the sole provider for his family. There is a danger of men's disappearing as actors in development.

Men have therefore become a development issue. But the responsibility for gender issues in organizations still rests overwhelmingly with women. Men do not often analyse or question their own dominance; gender equality is seen as women's struggle and men's response is reactive (either to resist or to make concessions graciously) rather than one of proactive involvement in creating gender equality. Clearly, a much broader and more substantive participation of men in processes of organizational change towards gender equality is essential. According to a male interviewee who is a staff member of the Swedish NGDO Forum Syd:[7]

> *Very few men are actually working with gender [in development NGDOs] and it's often women who formulate gender analyses and methods in the context of project or process support to women.... Isolated men working on gender issues end up carrying the burden of representing the oppressing sex ....*
>
> *Men must be made aware that they too are winners in a more equal society.Cooperation could be directed towards looking at problems of masculinity, ways of changing behaviour and attitudes, for instance giving assistance to organizations which give men opportunities to meet and discuss gender and new roles for men.*

Men need to be encouraged to see gender issues as something that concerns them as closely as it does women, so that they stop thinking of gender as coterminous with women. As we have noted elsewhere in this book, this needs to be done in a non-adversarial, inclusive way, focusing on common ground and interests, negotiating accommodation between differing interests, and highlighting the positive aspects of the gender change process for all concerned.

It is useful also to consider the value of strategic alliances between women and men on gender issues. Women have learned, over years of working in women's movements in their own countries or in partnership relations in NGDOs, that the category 'women' is by no means one undifferentiated block. It contains a huge variety of women and sometimes conflicting opinions, interests, and priorities. The same is true of men. Understanding this helps women to identify potential male allies, often among men who are themselves disadvantaged by the current system of gender/power relations, and also among men who choose to opt out of predominant stereotypes of masculinity.[8] Men as strategic allies can contribute much, for instance, through dialogue with other men who might be less willing to listen to women.

From the point of view of our roadmap, involving men in the process means that organizational analyses and diagnoses need to include men in a way which does not

## THE NICARAGUAN GROUP MEN AGAINST VIOLENCE AGAINST WOMEN

In 1993, men in Managua working with women organizing against male violence made a commitment to support women by forming a men's group to change men's attitudes and 'actively unlearn machismo'. The group's work centres on gender training for men, analysing and developing alternative models of masculinity, and educating men against male violence. They now have about 800 members and a training programme covering most of the country, working with peasant and other groups.

The group is an interesting example of how readiness to change is reached via a combination of factors. Factors leading to the establishment of the group included:

- a tradition of extreme machismo into which men are socialized from infancy; a society in which men are expected to face and to exercise violence;
- the politico-economic situation of poverty, unemployment (especially among men), and war in Nicaragua, contributing to rising violence against women and children;
- the presence of a large and very active women's mass organization (with support from the Sandinista government until 1990) which as early as 1980 was lobbying for legislation on responsible paternity and male violence;
- the positive impact of the women's movement on some men, providing support and legitimation for men who had come to realize (but had not admitted openly because of peer pressure) that machismo straitjackets and impoverishes men's lives as well as oppressing women;
- a culture of open discussion (community groups, women's groups, etc.) established during the Sandinista period as part of participatory democracy;
- growth of interest among Northern donor NGDOs in funding programmes with a strong gender component.[9]

assume that men are the norm, but turns the same critical spotlight on men's gender identities and interests as women's. Analysis needs to cover differences between men in the organization as well as differences between men and women and between different constituencies of women. Also, men are obviously key interlocutors in processes of building consensus and identifying allies. However, we must always keep in mind the extraordinary facility with which the dominant (in this case patriarchal) discourse asserts itself and coopts alternative discourses. As Sarah White remarks (Macdonald, 1994: 105): 'The original patterns of male and female identities do change, but in the new arrangement men still come out on top.' Women have to continue to guard against cosmetic changes which do not really affect the underlying unequal gender balance.

Nonetheless, if we are to bring men on board on the basis of their realization of their own self-interest in gender equality, we need to think in terms of maximizing their positive contribution rather than simply overcoming their resistance or 'coming out on top' ourselves. Many of the strategies outlined in chapters 7 and 8 apply specifically to working with men in this way.

### Bottom-up or top-down?

As we have already remarked, this framework is built on the assumption that the process envisaged is a bottom-up-driven process. Certainly, it is more likely that, within an organization, pressure for undertaking the change process on gender will come from below (staff members, women), although the internal mandate and resources may need to come from above. In the case of the Northern donor/Southern counterpart relationship, the process is often (but not always) driven from above (donor pressure or conditionality) but in alliance with sectors in the counterpart or its external context (women in the counterpart, women's organizations in the counterpart's country). In some cases, it is women in the counterpart or its region who have exerted the upward pressure for the change process on the donor or have supported women in the donor organization in their pressure for change.

However, as the matrix in chapter 2 (see 'Power, role, and personality') suggests, there may be a large subdominant group of people, particularly in large NG(D)Os, who, at the beginning of the process, have not yet made an analysis of the gender dynamics of their organization (or indeed of society in general). This group might well feel that the only stage at which they could intervene was the first, and that the rest of the process could be out of their hands, and even entirely management-led. Mechanisms of consultation would have to be put in place to make sure that people at all levels are involved actively. This would to a considerable extent depend on the role and attitudes of the change agent, but also on the support of top management. The bottom line is the willingness of senior managers to devote the necessary time and money to the change process.

On a more positive note, however, sharing and participation in the process are key. Again, the more people in the organization who are involved and 'own' the process, the more effective the process will be; so it is of prime importance to involve everyone in the organization.

Finally, transparency and accountability are a two-way street in this process. An organizational climate of openness, honesty, and accountability is, as we have noted, an important factor in establishing willingness to change the organization, and a prerequisite for securing a mandate for the change process. Moreover, the process itself should contribute to increasing transparency and accountability between different interest groups in the organization: staff and management, women and men, and – in the case of the donor/counterpart relationship – Northern donors and Southern counterparts.

### A note on leadership

Although these change processes must be participative and collective, good leadership is also an important factor. In particular, trainer–facilitators will need participative leadership qualities.

De Beuk (1995: no. 4) lists some desirable qualities of a leader. The good leader:

- *facilitates:* creates moments and conditions for information exchange; creates moments, procedures and opportunities for discussion and policy-making;
- *guards and controls:* ensures that decisions are taken; checks that what has been decided is put into practice, and if it is not, identifies what is necessary to ensure implementation;
- *stimulates and motivates:* makes sure that everyone is participating in discussion and decision-making; identifies what individuals and groups need to participate or to feel comfortable in the organization;
- *delegates:* leaves as much as possible to the people involved;
- *takes the power of decision if necessary:* in certain situations decision-making power needs to be exercised by the leader, for instance if the group cannot make a choice, or if discussion is being avoided in a situation where people or systems are dysfunctional.

However, these qualities contain their own contradictions, e.g. between controlling and delegating, or between facilitating/stimulating while always leaving open the possibility that the leader will take over decision-making if required. The challenge for the leader is to strike a good balance between the controlling, authoritarian, command-based elements of leadership and the guiding, nurturing, consultative elements.

It has been suggested by some that these contrasting qualities define 'masculine' and 'feminine' types of leadership respectively, and this dichotomy has become the basis for popular stereotypes of male and female styles of leadership and management (see chapter 1, 'Organizations and gender').

While it seems simplistic to gender-stereotype as 'feminine' qualities such as global vision, sensitivity, or the ability to express emotions, or as 'masculine' for instance firmness, a focus on goals, readiness to take risks, it is important to recognize that each of these qualities has its place. As ever, the challenge is to find the right combination or balance of different qualities – which will vary according to changing circumstances and players and the particular problem to be addressed.

## Donors and counterparts

In the case of Northern donor organizations working with Southern counterparts, this framework could clearly be used to carry through a process of organizational change within either a donor or a counterpart organization. However, donors should not intervene directly in the process if it is being carried out by counterparts. Donors need to understand the process, be able to see readiness to change, then dialogue with counterparts, perhaps with external facilitation. Donor staff can possibly be an ally to counterparts, but they may also be part of the problem. Donor agencies themselves, therefore, cannot play the role of the change agent in their counterparts' processes of change, as they are part of the external environment of counterpart organizations. In particular, the unequal nature of the donor/counterpart relationship, springing from the counterpart's financial dependence on the donor, militates against donors' acting as change agents or facilitators in their counterparts' processes of change.

Finally, the interdependence of changes occurring at donor and at counterpart level is also an important factor to be taken into account: applying the framework to a donor organization necessarily implies a change in its relationship with its counterparts. None of these processes is static, and none exists in a vacuum.

## Notes

1. The framework presented here is closely based on that presented at the 1995 *Eurostep* gender workshop by facilitators Aruna Rao and Wanjiru Kihoro. This, in turn, draws heavily on the BRAC Gender Program design as discussed in Rao and Kelleher 1995a and revised by Aruna Rao and David Kelleher in May 1996.

2. See Kelleher et al., 1996b: 26, 29.

3. Anne Marie Goetz, quoted in ibid.: 3.

4. This term was coined by David Kelleher.

5. List derived from presentation by Aruna Rao at *Eurostep* gender workshop 1995, based on Aruna Rao and David Kelleher, 'BRAC Gender Quality Action Learning program: evaluation design', 11 June 1995, mimeo. We are also indebted to this paper for other insights in this section.

6. See Introduction for definitions of the WID and GAD approaches.

7. Carl-Johan Smedeby, presentation at the *Eurostep* 1996 gender workshop, Oslo, 9–12 October 1996. A Swedish network of men working with gender issues in development cooperation was formed in 1996.

8. See Sarah White, 'Making men an issue: gender planning for the other half?', in Macdonald, 1994: 108.

9. Information given by Edgar Amador, coordinator of the men's group, during a visit to One World Action, London, November 1996.

# 7  Organizational culture, the change agent, and gender

Two elements which could be added to the framework for organizational change described in the last chapter are *organizational culture* and the *role of the change agent*. Organizational culture is one of the most important factors the change agent working in or with an organization has to deal with. In fact, particularly with regard to gender, profound, transforming change cannot really be achieved in an organization without changing organizational culture.[1]

## Organizational culture

Organizational culture is what we call the personality of an organization: if the organization's structure can be thought of as its body, its personality or soul is the way people deal with each other and the values and beliefs that are dominant. Organizational culture determines the conventions and unwritten rules of the organization, its norms of cooperation and conflict, its channels for exerting influence. Another way of describing organizational culture is as a collective mindset, or 'software of the mind'.

'Hofstede's onion' is a useful tool for understanding the deeper cultural aspects of an organization (see diagram on following page). The first description of an organization you are likely to receive will be the 'official version' – the portrait the organization (and particularly its top management) wants to convey, through its publicity, information brochures, and publications. This can be thought of as the 'skin' of the onion. Under this skin, however, aspects of organizational culture can be seen as arranged in 'layers', from the most superficial outward signifiers of the organization to its most deeply-held – and not always easily discernible – central values. The superficial outer layers can be very significant pointers to the real values of the organization. As Hofstede's onion shows, an organization's culture can be described in terms of several factors.

- Its symbols: the size and look of the building that houses it, the furnishing of offices at different levels in the organization, the clothes staff wear, the cars they drive, etc.

- Its 'heroes' and 'villains': which leaders or former leaders are 'worshipped', which are used to describe catastrophes? These can say a lot about how you have to behave to be accepted in the organization. An organization may venerate, for instance, a founding director, who may be mythologized into embodying the organization's real values; if its anti-heroes are the nine-to-five bureaucrats, this is a clue to the kind of behaviour expected of staff.

**Hofstede's onion: a model of organizational culture**

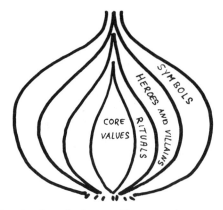

- Its rituals: whether staff eat together or not, how they greet each other, whether (and with whom) people talk about their private affairs; how meetings are organized; the celebration of organizational 'feast-days', staff members' birthdays, weddings, departures from the organization, etc.

All these layers overlay and envelop, but also provide clues to:

- The values of the organization, the fundamental principles and beliefs that underlie its practice: these determine what is really thought important and desirable and what is devalued in the organization. Be aware here of the distinction between 'aspired-to' and 'integrated' values. Aspired-to values are the values which people say are important to the organization, whether or not this is borne out in practice. Integrated values are the real values: the heart of the culture. There can be a big gap between aspired-to and integrated values, and this occurs especially when dealing with gender, where you may find politically correct rhetoric but no real intention to integrate gender equality fully into the organization's culture. There can also be different values, or different-sized gaps between aspired-to and integrated values, at different levels, or among different sectors, of the organization.

*How does an organization's culture develop?*
To understand how the culture of an organization has developed – how the organization reached the position it is in today – it is also important to analyse its origin and history. An organization that was born out of protest or struggle against a dominant system, for instance, can find it difficult to adapt to new ideas and a new analysis, since its initial, defining posture originated from struggle. Though this may have been useful in the beginning, it can be a hindrance if it persists. Strongly ideologized organizations tend to have rigid views of right and wrong; this makes it difficult for them to adapt to a new analysis, but once they are convinced their strong emotional involvement can be mobilized again. The change agent needs to try to understand the organization within

its own history and context, the traumas it may have gone through, which influence the way it is dealing with change now.

The organizational culture, in particular its openness to free communication, access to information, and innovative practices, also offers clues as to whether the organization is a learning organization or not. A capacity for learning at the institutional level is a prerequisite for organizational change.

### Gender and organizational culture

Theorists of gender and organizations have left us in no doubt that the ways organizations work mirror the ways society at large works. Power, in organizations as in society, is gendered (Acker, 1992; Goetz, 1995: 5). This means that sexism and gender inequality are as firmly embedded in the structure and culture of organizations as they are in the structure and culture of societies. Thus, intentionally or not, the dominant organizational culture of even the most progressive mixed organization is very likely to be masculine and to discriminate against women.

Integrating gender means change – cross-cutting, pervasive change, which should affect all aspects of an organization's policy and practice. So the relation between gender and organizational culture is a logical and necessary one. The case studies presented in earlier chapters of this book show clearly how changes in structure and procedures (increasing gender parity in the organization or setting new targets for women's participation, the introduction of gender-responsible structures, increasing resources), while undoubtedly valuable in certain contexts and for certain periods of time, have not by themselves achieved the real sea-change that is necessary to shift the gender-based balance of power. Changes in structure and procedures are always reversible, revocable, subject to changes in other factors (money, leadership, energy, external politico-economic circumstances, etc.). Changing organizational culture so that gender equality is understood and accepted as a core value of the organization is the only real guarantee of permanent, meaningful change.

## The change agent

An agent of change working in or with an organization needs three things:
- modest aims combined with ambition;
- an understanding of the culture of the organization;
- flexibility as regards strategy.

*Modest aims and ambition.* As a change agent, you must be simultaneously modest and ambitious. Modest, because changing the personality – the 'soul' – of an organization is very difficult and painful. Many people spend a long time and much money in therapy and still the changes can be very small. Nevertheless, you must also be ambitious, for if you don't believe in this process of change, in the possibility to mobilize the healthy nucleus that exists in every organization, who else will?

This combination of modesty and ambition means stimulating and rewarding activities and persons heading in the desired direction, while not expecting dramatic results in a very short time or raising expectations unrealistically high.

Another consequence is that the change agent must be a motivator. An external consultant, even though s/he is asked (and paid) to support an organization in this process of change, nevertheless usually finds that s/he has to motivate those taking part. This is even more important when you are yourself part of the organization, with special responsibility for gender work. Part of the game is that the gender responsibles have to motivate people around them, even though this is not mentioned in any contract. And they have to give extra energy all the time, being aware that in the end enough momentum must have been generated in the organization for it to continue on its own.

*From understanding to change.* The change agent needs to understand not only the features of organizational culture outlined above – its system of rituals, values and beliefs – but also its structures and practice. These give clues to how it can be changed. They should also be analysed in historical terms: understanding of past changes helps in planning future ones. What to keep from the past, what to get rid of? Thus, the change agent must try to analyse the following factors.

- 'What business are we in?' Do those within the organization share a vision of the organization's core business?

- Its history: just as with a person, an organization is shaped by its life events, and goes through life cycles. Is it a young (new) organization or an old established one? What traumas and crises has it gone through? How did it react to them, and how does that still influence the way this organization is dealing with things?

- Its structures and procedures, and how they have evolved (by consensus, top–down, bottom–up, etc.);

- Its vertical relationships: what is the relationship between the leadership and the 'shop floor' like?

- Its horizontal relationships: how do staff functions relate to the line? How do different departments relate to each other? Are there formal or informal linkages between departments?

- Internal/external interaction (stakeholders context): threats or opportunities from outside (from partners, funding sources, political supporters or opponents) will produce reactions on the inside.

The change agent also needs to understand how the culture of an organization sustains itself. In general, culture sustains and reproduces itself through socialization of

## THE EXPERIMENT OF THE MONKEYS

This experiment demonstrates how culture maintains itself in an organization through socialization and giving a high value to conformity.

A caged group of monkeys was confronted with a bunch of bananas on a platform. When they tried to take them they were hosed down, so, as monkeys are afraid of water, they left the bananas alone. Each time they tried to reach the bananas, the same thing happened, so they stopped trying.

Then one of the monkeys was replaced by a 'new' one: he saw the bananas and tried to get them ... and was attacked by the other monkeys. He left the bananas. A second 'old' monkey was replaced by a new one and when this new one tried to get at the bananas he too was attacked by the others, the first 'new' monkey (who himself had been attacked earlier) taking the lead.

This continued until all the monkeys had been replaced by new monkeys: the group no longer contained any monkeys that had ever been hosed down. The water installation was removed, but still the monkeys never dared to take the bunch of bananas: that was 'not done'. (De Beuk, 1995: no. 3)

newcomers – 'that's the way we do things around here' – and through selection, seen for instance in the tendency to employ a person just like the one who just left. On the face of it, it always seems easier not to change than to change. Culture is often sustained, also, by the expectations of outsiders, who may be reacting to an 'old' or outdated image of the organization. The organization has not only to change but to convince everyone else that it has changed!

Thus, the change agent working on gender must try to:

- *Be encouraging about what's positive* related to the gender goals. Rewarding the positive is a better strategy than punishing the negative! The change agent, together with the organization, should be able to define which aspects of the organization are positive and which negative as regards gender equality. Some values which tend to be seen as positive – particularly by NGDOs – such as the ethic of overwork, self-exploitation and ignoring material rewards, turn out to be negative for women (and for both sexes, especially parents).

- *Get commitment from the top levels* of the organization, whose behaviour should be a model for the rest of the organization. There should be a clear mission with a concrete goal. The top management should be involved. Change may be proposed from within, quite often as the result of interaction with the outside world, but top

- Explain how incorporating the gender dimension does not necessarily add to people's workload, and can actually make their work easier.

- Emphasize the PR value of gender: as the interviews in chapter 2 show, many managers are already aware that a good track record on gender issues is good for the organization's image and reputation, in the case of donor agencies not only with the European public but with counterparts. Encourage this attitude.

- In the case of gender activists working within donor agencies, stress that counterparts want and expect gender sensitivity in donor agencies, especially if the donor is pushing for gender sensitivity with counterparts; present this as a democracy/accountability issue, appealing to the donor organization's founding values.

- For donor organizations promoting greater attention to gender with counterparts, adopt a positive rather than a punitive approach: encouraging and rewarding good performance is obviously better than sanctioning poor performance. Care must be taken, however, that this does not tip over into conditionality and is not seen as such by counterparts; some kind of separation between funding and support for the process of incorporating a gender perspective is advisable (see Eade, 1991). Supportive training and learning activities could include:
  - organizing workshops on gender-sensitive partnership counterparts, including staff of both mixed and women-only organizations;
  - holding an annual workshop on gender (e.g. on monitoring and evaluation);
  - promoting a wide discussion across counterpart organizations on values, leading to training on gender, using evaluation and the experience of local consultants.

## Organization-specific strategies

Once the organization has accepted the need to work towards gender sensitivity and gender equality, there is an array of strategies it can deploy to carry this aim forward. In any organization, strategies (of greater or lesser complexity) might include:
- revisiting the mission statement and objectives;
- stakeholder analysis;
- policy formulation;
- strategic planning;
- training;
- allocating budgets;
- setting targets for reaching gender parity in staffing at various levels;
- altering recruitment criteria and procedures;
- restructuring departments to mainstream gender;
- appointing one or more gender responsibles;
- making the workplace and workstyle more woman-friendly in various ways;

- devising and implementing gender equality monitoring and evaluation mechanisms;
- securing the commitment of top management to change towards greater gender equality.

The list could go on and on. More specifically in relation to work with counterpart organizations, strengthening dialogue about gender is key, but, again, the commitment of management to gender equality as an essential factor in true and sustainable development, and the allocation of adequate resources to support change undertaken by counterparts, are crucial.

An early start is important both in work within any organization, North or South, and in partnership with counterparts. Gender issues really need to be introduced from the outset, at the strategic planning stage; trying to graft gender onto a project or programme that has already been planned in its key aspects is counterproductive. Strategic planning should be done from a gender perspective, thus bringing gender in at the very beginning with inputs into the definition of strategic objectives for the upcoming period by different departments. Allies can be strengthened in the course of the strategic planning exercise, too.

However, these are extremely general points. The strategies which can be universally recommended are very few; in practice there are as many strategies as there are organizations. There is no one thing to be done; rather, there is an array of interventions which can be used in combination or separately, at different times, with different interlocutors in the organization.

The most important thing is that strategies for installing gender equality at the heart of an organization should fit the organization's own perceived needs. Resistance to the introduction of gender (on the part of both men and women in the organization) often springs from resentment of what is seen as an attempt to corral the organization and the people in it into some kind of rigid mould, a straitjacket of 'political correctness'. Much of this resentment can be dispelled by an approach that is specific to each organization and is designed around needs identified by the organization itself. Stages 1 and 2 of the roadmap in chapter 6 are relevant here. The Gender Route, a new initiative currently being undertaken by the Dutch NGDO Novib and some of its counterparts, aims to offer just such an organization-specific approach. It is described at the end of this chapter.

## Dealing with resistance

It is easy to draw up long checklists of possible strategies for making an organization more gender-sensitive. But what happens when it comes to implementing them? Most people working in NGOs are already working very hard, if not overworking. Yet we are telling them that achieving organizational change necessarily involves everyone in the organization. People are bound to ask, does this mean extra work for them? Why should they do it? Where will they find the time? Is this gender business really necessary, really worth the effort? As some of the interviews in chapter 3 show, the expression of resistance to change is never far below the surface, although the resistance itself may be deeply rooted, even subconscious. It may appear disguised as ignorance or mystification, a claim not to know which is really an unwillingness to know or to think about the issue. Or – particularly in organizations which have some years of experience in gender work and a strong gender team – it may surface as gender fatigue or complacency: 'we've done a lot already, we can't keep beating the gender drum for ever'.

Resistance to change can be buried deep, and can be built on even a small or trivial event. It can arise in individuals because the basic ideas are not understood; because the individual is, or feels, neglected as a person; because of lack of equality (the more powerful fear losing their privileges, the less powerful fear that change could only worsen their situation); because of buried experiences leading to a vague, ill-defined hostility. The organizational culture of self-sacrifice, overwork, and disregard for material rewards that characterizes many – perhaps most – development NGOs may in this respect unwittingly contribute to resistance to change. The more people feel they only give to the organization and get nothing back, the more threatened they feel by the introduction of new concepts, such as diversity and gender, that seem to require yet more of them and promise no easy answers or short-term rewards.

The following are some strategies for confronting personal resistance (the preceding list of strategies for encouraging acceptance of gender issues can also be adapted to this use).

- Clarify the concept of gender; but also look critically at our own vocabulary as gender experts, which can be confusing and mystifying. Gender is really a very simple concept, a matter of common sense, and we should be careful that our discourse does not make it seem more complicated, obscure, or excluding than it is.

- Don't pretend that resistance doesn't exist: explore people's fears and doubts sincerely and seriously. But don't waste time on lost causes. The extent of people's potential interest in a given issue can be represented as a pie, as shown in the illustration.

We tend all too often to concentrate most strongly or even exclusively on winning over the 'very negatives', who pose the greatest challenge but also offer the slimmest chance of success. Perhaps we should be abandoning the lost causes and concentrating our persuasive efforts on the 'neutral/doubtful' and 'don't know' categories, while at the same time nurturing the 'positives' and 'very positives', building on their support and using it to buttress the efforts of winning over the waverers. Listening only to negative feedback is demoralizing and disempowering.

- Another point about morale: be realistic, and don't set expectations too high: disappointment is much greater in the event of failure, and that makes it much harder to try again. Remember that the process of change is gradual and not linear; build setbacks, delays and digressions into your expectations!

**The 'interest pie'**

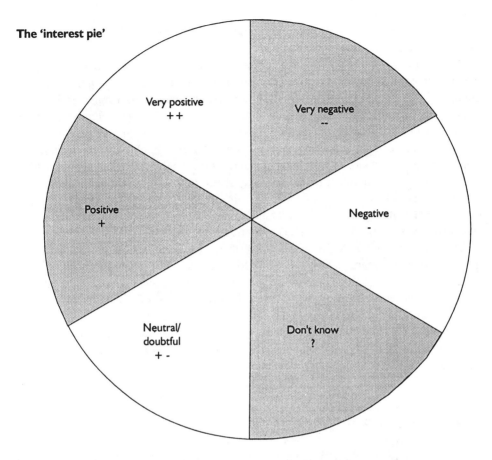

## Confronting double standards

As is clear from the *Eurostep* gender workshop, many organizations still have double standards on gender. This may surface in the form of political correctness, in which the rhetoric of gender equality is highly developed but not much is done in practice, or where policy exists but is not implemented (for reasons which are never ascribed to lack of commitment to gender equality). For example, a public service might have a policy of equal opportunities and even targets for number of female staff at professional or managerial levels, but effectively exclude women from applying for jobs by setting gender-biased qualifying examinations, or by institutionalizing a workstyle requiring frequent travel or transfers of posting at short notice.[2]

The donor/counterpart relationship is especially vulnerable to the problem of double standards, given the inevitably unequal relationship between Northern donors and Southern counterparts. Many donors pay close attention to gender issues in their work with counterparts but little or none where their own organization is concerned. Resource constraints are often cited as the reason, and it is argued that, in an adverse economic climate, work with the counterparts must always come first. It is important to point out that this is a false dichotomy: promoting gender fairness abroad and practising it at home *must* go hand in hand.

A key strategy in this situation is to ensure that internal organizational development is firmly integrated into the organization's implementation of its gender policy, so that attention is given to the organization itself, not just to counterparts. Counterparts are increasingly unwilling to accept donors' demands that they devise and implement a gender policy while the donors themselves show evidence of continuing gender inequality, for example in staffing parity. It could be useful to play into the organization's identity as a donor, highlighting counterpart interest in its internal gender work and stressing that accountability is a two-way street. In cases where directors tend to listen more closely to counterparts than to their own staff, pressure from counterparts on the donor's management, even if it comes indirectly via reports from the donor's field officers or desk officers, can be productive.

The Belgian NGDO NCOS, which deliberately postponed beginning work on gender with counterparts until it had achieved satisfactory internal progress on developing policy and good practice on gender, found it especially beneficial to all parties to learn from counterparts. In 1995 it invited about 20 of its counterparts – a mixed group, not just the gender-aware counterparts – to Belgium to discuss what they wanted NCOS to do with respect to campaigning, education, and programme work. Such an exchange of experiences on an equal basis can be very empowering for counterparts.


## Strategic location of change agents

Each organization should analyse the most strategic location for change agents on gender in the light of its history and its current needs. A gender focal point needs to be easily accessible and user-friendly for colleagues, but also able to protect itself from being swamped with sole responsibility for everything concerning women in the whole organization. Basically, the gender team is a pressure group within the organization, often directed especially towards lobbying management, facilitating access to and organizational learning about innovative gender practices.

As remarked earlier (chapter 1), a combined strategy of locating gender responsibles or experts in a decentralized way throughout the organization (with the aim of facilitating the implementation of gender-equal policies throughout) plus a strong gender team with direct access to senior management, is probably the most effective model. However, each organization will have its own version of this combination, and some smaller organizations may not have sufficient resources for both elements. The most strategic location for the gender change agents is also likely to change over time as the organization's policy and practice change. The location of change agents affects not only gender work with counterparts or target groups but gender in internal organizational development, and slightly different strategies may be required for these two different focuses. This division may seem somewhat artificial, but in many larger organizations it may be inevitable, since their internal development and externally focused work are dealt with by different departments. For example, the large British NGDO Oxfam UK/I for many years worked on gender equality on two tracks: one consisted of work inside the organization (starting with in-house daycare for staff members' pre-school children and a policy of equal opportunities), while the other strand involved work directed towards programme outcomes. The two strands were not linked, were implemented by different departments, and were based on different concepts of equality. This dichotomy points up the importance of linking the goals and agenda on gender and organizational change with the strategic objectives of the organization as a whole,[5] for instance by establishing mechanisms of regular communication between different departments dealing with gender-related issues.

## Developing a woman-friendly organizational culture

Making an organization's culture friendly to women involves challenging male dominance. Women need to move as freely and comfortably in the organizational medium as men do: to reclaim a cliché usually uttered as criticism, women need to be able to act 'as if they owned the place'. To achieve this, an organizational culture and structures of mutual support for women need to be built, so that women can feel they are not isolated individuals but a potentially powerful group. This may mean setting up a staff women's group or developing an existing one; allocating a physical space such as a common-room exclusively to women; holding seminars or other events (women-only and for both sexes) on gender issues; or other strategies.

A valuable tool for empowerment for women is a close knowledge and a critical analysis from a gender perspective of the organization's rules and procedures, for example its statutes, contracts, terms and conditions of work. If women are able to work from an informed position to expose the gender biases in such documents, they are better equipped to argue for change. It is also important to analyse the informal structures which hamper the proper implementation of formal structures. This may require external support or facilitation by someone who is not immersed in the organization's culture.

Practical strategies to make the organization more friendly to women, and to parents and carers of both sexes, include reorganizing working hours to allow workers to attend to family responsibilities; policies on maternity and paternity leave; childcare facilities on site; planning which gives adequate notice of trips abroad, and possibly spreading travel responsibilities more widely among staff. Many organizations have already given attention to some of these features. However, sometimes changes are made ad hoc, as the need arises, rather than as a matter of policy. This is obviously dangerous. If an organization waits until one of its workers becomes pregnant before it works out a policy and procedures for maternity/paternity leave, it will probably already have lost valuable human resources in the women who will not apply for posts with it because it has made no provision for its workers' becoming parents. Alternatively, women work-ing in the organization may either avoid becoming pregnant until they are ready to leave, or leave if they become pregnant. This kind of self-selection allows the organiza-

## CASE STUDY: THE GENDER ROUTE

'The Gender Route' is a joint learning process for Novib, its counterparts and a pool of consultants on the integration of a gender perspective into development work. It emphasizes the need for a *triangle of gender learning*. The project was initiated by Novib in 1995 and will be completed in the year 2000, when an evaluation of its impact will be undertaken. One of the key activities in this process is to give special support to about 35 mixed counterpart organizations distributed over the continents of Asia, Africa, and Latin America, including some international network organizations, enabling them to define, develop, and implement their own gender policy.

### Background to the project

In the past Novib has developed and implemented different strategies and instruments with regard to the integration of a gender approach in counterpart organizations. Some of these are:[4]
- inclusion of gender-relevant issues in terms of reference for monitoring and evaluation;
- requirement for consultants to be gender-sensitive, and inclusion of at least one woman and one gender expert in teams of consultants;
- gender checklist for project approval;
- facilitation of linking and learning opportunities for counterparts, e.g. workshops, standing gender working groups with regular meetings, and exchange visits;
- stressing Novib's key interest in gender issues during counterpart conferences and workshops;
- discussing gender issues during field visits;
- integrating a gender perspective in country and regional policy documents;
- funding at least one, and possibly two, women's organizations per country.

Novib can confirm that these instruments have contributed to putting gender on the agenda in many counterpart organizations. However, putting gender on the agenda is just the first step leading up to a process of dynamic change requiring tailor-made support and activities. Novib has found that a pioneer group of counterparts are making the shift from good intentions, or perhaps an occasional women's project or gender training, towards identifying implications for the organization as a whole. They are in the process of making a gender perspective part and parcel of everyday practice and increasingly express the need for guidance and support, for example in the form of backstopping support from consultants.

On the basis of these observations Novib set out to obtain more insight and information on organizational dynamics of counterpart organizations and the comparative effectiveness of the different interventions, strategies, and instruments. The broader aim of this exercise is to contribute actively to equal rights and opportunities for women and men. It is against this background that in 1995 Novib decided to launch a project entitled 'The Gender Route'.

## Objectives and content

The objective is to answer the following questions:
- How can Novib, in its role as a donor, best support and promote gender learning and good gender practice among counterpart organizations?

- How do counterpart organizations assess Novib's gender practice?

- What minimum gender criteria should Novib apply to its total pool of counterpart organizations?

Thirty-five mixed NGOs, out of a total of some 800 counterpart organizations, have been requested to participate in the project. They were selected on the grounds of their interest in taking gender issues forward and their long-term relationship with Novib. For pragmatic reasons, the country or region in question also needs to have, or to be able to build up, sufficient capacity in the form of expert advisers.

The Gender Route itself is a three- to four-year process involving local consultants facilitating a gender self-diagnosis of the organization. A precondition is that the self-diagnosis covers the internal organization, its network of external relations, and the level of products and activities in relation to target groups. On the basis of the self-diagnosis each counterpart defines and follows its own route, appropriate to its own situation. The project is intended to be sufficiently flexible and variable to encompass the needs and contexts of organizations of different natures, sizes, and compositions, with different remits, in different national and cultural contexts, and at different stages in the integration of gender. Another key feature is that regular moments where counterparts exchange and compare results among themselves (peer comparisons) and with Novib are built in.

For Novib, the project is intended to increase knowledge about good practice both in terms of promoting gender sensitivity and gender equality with counterparts, and making the right funding decisions. It will share its findings with other organizations, including donor organizations, and thereby facilitate a multiplier and spinoff effect.

## Phases of the process

After the counterpart has agreed to participate, the Route can be broken down into four phases.

1. An analysis or inventory of the current state of play with respect to gender and the relationship between the counterpart and Novib on this issue (1996).

2. A gender self-diagnosis of the organization's structure, culture, relationships with other organizations, product, activities, programmes, etc., carried out as a participatory learning exercise by staff and facilitated by external consultants if necessary; followed by identifying objectives, defining criteria for evaluation, and drawing up an activity plan (1997).

3. Counterpart implementation of the tailor-made activity plan (1997–2000). Possible activities could be:
- research and baseline studies on (context-specific) gender relations;
- increasing the number of women staff at higher and middle levels of the organization;
- on-the-job training, exchanges, or traineeships;
- developing or strengthening external linkages with women's organizations, centres of expertise, or peer organizations with the objective of linking, learning, and comparing the results of interventions and activities.

4. Evaluation of the process (2000):
- individual evaluations of participating counterparts, focusing on the objectives and indicators as formulated in 1997 (self-diagnosis);
- an evaluation of the overall objectives of the Gender Route Project.

Coordination and information exchange between Novib, the counterparts, and consultants will continue throughout the duration of the project.

Although the Gender Route is a pilot project being implemented with only a small proportion of Novib's counterpart organizations, its findings and experience should open the way for a much larger learning process regarding good practice, what works and what doesn't work in gender interventions, which strategies can be replicated in a variety of settings and which are uniquely applicable. The findings will make a distinction between good organizational practice in general and good donor practice, such as that vis à vis counterparts.

---

## Notes

1. This list and the following list on confronting resistance are based on discussions among participants at the 1995 *Eurostep* gender workshop.

2. Macdonald, 1995: 44–6.

3. See Kelleher et al., 1996b: 36, 40.

4. See the articles by A. Papma and E. Sprenger in Macdonald, 1994a, section IV.

# 9  Measuring progress

As we follow our roadmap of organizational change, how can we measure how far along the road we have come? How will we know when we have arrived? Can we identify any general indicators of good practice? This chapter looks at monitoring and evaluating processes of organizational change which aim at greater gender equality and more gender-sensitive practice in organizations.

## Organizational change as a permanent process

It should be recognized from the outset that this kind of monitoring and evaluation must be a permanent, ongoing process. The dynamic of change in organizations and their external environments means that indicators and their application change all the time. Certain indicators are relevant at certain times and in certain places, but not all at once. Organizations themselves consist of people who come and go and who change as individuals. They have life cycles, and gender work in organizations also has its life cycle. The kind of gender intervention appropriate at one moment in an organization's life cycle might be quite unsuitable at another.

Expectations also change during an organization's life cycle. The survey of Novib staff mentioned in the previous chapter found that, although 83% thought the affirmative action policy had been a success and 95% wanted to see it continued, 71% of women and 50% of men were dissatisfied with the organization's level of gender equality. These figures suggest that expectations rise precisely because of success. As people get more, they become more aware of what else is possible. As standards rise, fresh challenges come into view. So, side by side with great satisfaction, there is ever-renewed dissatisfaction with the distance still to be travelled and the apparent remoteness of the new horizons revealed from the perspective of each new height scaled.

Thus, evaluation becomes a continuous, cyclical process of learning and improving the gender quality of the organization. Processes of evaluation and change lead into one another. Since gender work is ongoing there can be no argument for setting up a gender structure that will perform a particular task (such as formulating a policy) and then disappear. There needs to be a mechanism that guarantees ongoing monitoring, quality control, ensuring the fit between policy and practice, and developing policy and practice to keep up with each new change in circumstances.

## Quality versus quantity: the problem with numbers

The easiest way of evaluating the success or failure of a development programme or intervention is in terms of quantifiable results: numbers of people to whom a service is delivered, areas of land cultivated, amounts of crops or artefacts produced, what it all costs, and so on. Many development organizations, most often large or hierarchical organizations, tend to define their achievements largely in these terms, in terms of setting and meeting numerical targets. They concentrate on service delivery, on getting the maximum amount of some commodity (not necessarily a tangible one – it can be literacy, or primary health care, or information, or gender training) to a given target population. This target-driven orientation is buttressed by the increasingly common emphasis on efficiency and cost-effectiveness in the language of development mana-gers. Northern NGDOs' public information and advertising often stress the quantitative – 'your contribution of just $10 can feed two families for a week' (but on what? and who in the family gets the food?) – presumably on the assumption that this concept is easy for people who are not development experts to grasp. Fixed funding periods also favour quantitative rather than qualitative measures of performance: significant changes in attitude or institutional behaviour may need longer than two or three years to become apparent and to consolidate themselves as regular practice rather than one-off events, so it is more bureaucratically satisfying to evaluate results in terms of training days held, pieces of research done, issues of a bulletin published.

This is a basis for evaluating performance that sits uncomfortably with broader gender equality objectives of changing the relationship of power between men and women in the direction of greater equality and the ability to negotiate and agree on the needs of both men and women. Some would argue that, particularly where cross-cutting or all-pervasive issues such as gender are concerned, setting any but the broadest of targets for performance (e.g. for the number of counterparts expected to have undertaken some concrete action on gender before the year 2000) is not particularly useful or appropriate. However, it should be possible to arrive at a balance of quantitative and qualitative measurements of progress. As Rao and Kelleher note (1995a: 72):

> *if you want to deepen the quality of the program and build a greater responsiveness to members (particularly female), you need to balance the target culture with a concern for quality of program and its impacts on empowerment of women.*
>
> *This does not mean ignoring targets like the number of loans made or the amount of money loaned. It means adding other measurements like the percentage of women who retain control over income or the numbers of women who become more influential as a result of income generation. It also means facing the issue of perhaps decreasing the target for loan disbursement in order to allow staff to focus on increasing the impact of the program on women's empowerment.*

Some donor agencies have found it useful to set targets for a number of anticipated results: the percentage of women's organizations among their counterparts, the percentage of credits which go to women in a specific sector, or (within an organization) the number of women trained, or the number of men trained in gender issues; but they stress that meeting this kind of target is only part of the story when it comes to more gender-sensitive practice, just as increasing the number of women staff members or managers is only part of the process of making our own organizations more gender-equal.

Chapter 6 (stage 6) lists qualitative indicators to use in assessing organizational change from a gender perspective: new knowledge and skills gained, changes in attitude, better working relationships. These things cannot be counted, but they are crucial indicators of progress or lack of it. However, quality is certainly much harder to measure than quantity. Criteria are more fluid; they vary with cultural and other factors. Relevant qualitative indicators have to be identified within each project or organization, specifically for that project or organization, and negotiated among different groups of stakeholders: donors, counterpart NGOs and grassroots beneficiaries, women and men may all have different criteria. Easy checklists of universally applicable evaluation criteria cannot be expected – indeed, they should be regarded with suspicion. Evaluating improvements in quality requires greater expertise and sensitivity on the part of the evaluators and greater trust and transparency between counterpart and donor. It also takes more time and therefore more resources, and sometimes a change in approach. Often an evaluator from a donor agency visiting a counterpart organization doesn't see the gender quality of the counterpart because the visit is too short for the evaluator to talk to everyone and she talks only to the counterpart's managers. What is the solution: to demand longer visits or fewer counterparts, or to seek an alternative measurement and evaluation procedure in which the counterpart's ongoing self-evaluation plays a greater part?

## Gender parity and gender commitment

Nowhere is the quality/quantity dilemma sharper than in the question of gender parity in an organization. There is evidence that some people in NGDOs (and more broadly) still think gender equality can be measured in terms of the number of women in an organization or a project: as some of the interviews presented in chapter 2 reveal, for some male colleagues, increasing 'the numerical participation of women at all levels in the projects' was enough. While there is no denying that the presence of more women at decision-making and especially top management levels in an organization is desirable for greater gender equality, in fact research has shown that once a critical mass of about 30–35% women in the organization, including at decision-making levels, has been achieved the organization as a whole becomes more accountable to the specific needs and interests of women. It is, however, important that the larger presence of women is matched by a commitment to making the organization right for women, putting gender policy into practice and influencing others to do so – and by the resources decision-makers are able to mobilize for implementing gender policies. We have mentioned above, in chapter 5, the pitfalls and obstacles that can affect a woman manager's ability to deliver gender-equal policies and practice, however senior her position. For a commitment to gender equality to be *structural*, not contingent upon the personalities and talents of powerful individuals in the organization, there must be a commitment to it at the very top levels, involving a willingness to look critically and creatively at the quality and function of management (not just its composition), to learn from best practice and to allocate adequate resources for the process.

At the bottom line, the difference between quantitative and qualitative indicators of progress is fundamentally the difference between access and control, a question of the degree to which a gender intervention increases the possibilities of *transforming* gender relations in the organization rather than simply making more or different things available to women.

## Guidelines for a gender assessment of an organization

The aim of these guidelines is to assist with the process of assessing an organization in all its aspects from a gender perspective. First, some definitions.

- A focus on gender rather than women implies not looking at 'women' and women's issues in isolation but recognizing the different needs and interests of women and men in the context of power relations between them.

- A gender analysis of an organization examines the processes and interventions in and by the organization in terms of their effects on women, men and the relationships between women and men. It explicitly recognizes the unequal gender relations between men and women in society.

- Gender equality means equality between women and men at various levels: equal material *welfare*, equal *access* to resources and opportunities, a *value* system based on the belief in equality, equal *participation* in decision-making, and equal *control* over resources and benefits.[1]

### How to use the questionnaire

An organization's commitment to gender equality must be analysed in terms of the organization's mission/goal and objective, policy, strategy, activities, internal structure and systems, organizational culture, and external context. These broad headings are used in the questionnaire which follows. A number of sample questions are given under each heading. However, this list should be considered as a guideline only, not as an all-embracing, exhaustive checklist in which questions can be answered by a simple 'yes' or 'no'. A number of other questions could easily be used as alternatives or additionally. Clearly, not all the questions will apply equally to all organizations. The selection of questions will have to reflect the size, complexity and history of the organization concerned. Given that organizations are constantly changing, certain questions might be more relevant than others at particular moments.

The questionnaire is intended to stimulate a deeper examination involving discussion and analysis of organizations and gender. This is the reason for questions such as: Why are things the way they are? Have they always been like that? The aim to indicate the areas and issues to which attention ought to be given when assessing how far an organization has progressed on the road to becoming a more gender-aware and gender-equal organization.

There is no ready-made recipe for this process, as each organization is unique and has its own characteristics in terms of identity, size, age, organizational phase of development, context and cultural setting. Organizations in different regions of the world will carry out the journey towards gender sensitivity in very different ways and at very different paces; NGOs and grassroots groups will also differ in their experience and interpretation of the process.

The questions do not necessarily deal with gender issues alone. Information regarding overall organizational functioning and context is a critical part of a gender analysis of an organization.

## Core business of the organization

*Mission, goal, objective (the purpose of, and rationale behind, the organization's existence)*
- Does the organization have a clearly defined mission which enables it to assess its achievements in comparison to what it has defined as the rationale for its existence?

- Does the gender vision/perspective of the organization acknowledge the existence of power inequalities between men and women? To which aspects of gender inequality does it refer: welfare, access, values, participation, control?

- Are the mission statement and vision based on a thorough analysis of the context, including a perspective on gender inequality?

- Is the organization also aware of what is *not* its mission?

- Does the organization have a convincing rationale making clear why it is the best (perhaps unique) organization to carry out its mission (as opposed to any other organization)? In other words, is the organization aware of what would be qualitatively missing if it were not there?

- Is the mission written down and/or known by the organization's members, staff at different levels, and board? Is there evidence of their commitment to it?

- Is there evidence of support and commitment to the organization's mission and existence by beneficiaries, providing legitimacy and relevance?

*Intervention strategy (strategy of the organization, defining how it intends to achieve its mission/goal)*

- Has the organization translated its mission into clear, defined goals and ways and means of achieving these goals, specifying long- and short-term objectives and a plan of activities?

- Does the organization have specific objectives regarding gender in relation to its overall mission?

- Does the gender policy inform the overall policies of the organization? The policies of specific sectors?

- Does the gender policy inform intervention strategies in general?

- Does the gender policy include intervention strategies with regard to the beneficiaries of activities, the organization itself, and the external context of the organization?

- Are the different elements of the gender policy consistent with each other?

- Does the gender policy of the organization recognize the diversity of needs and interests among women (socioeconomic, ethnicity, cultural identity, sexuality, age, religion) among women?

- Do the intervention strategies of the organization emphasize women-specific, men-specific and/or mixed activities? What are the advantages and disadvantages of the different strategies pursued in terms of addressing gender inequalities?

- Has the organization developed the capacity to recognize and handle resistance to addressing gender issues?

*Products (the activities, services, programmes, output of the organization)*

- Why and how have the products been selected by the organization? Have women among the beneficiaries influenced the particular choices made?

- Was an inventory made of the interests and needs of women prior to the design of the organization's products, taking into account women's workload, available time, education and skills?

- Do the women among the beneficiaries value the products and see them as a priority?

- Do the products contribute to increased gender equality in terms of welfare, access, participation, ideology and control? In other words, what is the impact of the organization's products for men and for women in terms of:
  - material well-being, workload, division of tasks and responsibilities;
  - access to resources, information and education/training;
  - participation in decision-making regarding their productive, reproductive and community/political tasks;
  - images and values concerning femininity and masculinity, self-respect, legal status;
  - control over resources, information and benefits?

- Do the products of the organization contribute towards a change in macro-policies and/or legislation with regard to gender inequalities?

## Structure, systems and resources (also known as processes, procedures)

The structure of an organization refers to the relative positions of the parts of the organization, the division of tasks, responsibility and authority. Systems refer to the way in which various processes, decision-making and flows take place within the organization. Systems include both formal and informal elements.

### Structure
- Are there adequate and effective mechanisms for coordination and consultation among the various parts of the organization?

- Do these mechanisms include coordination and consultation with regard to the implementation of the gender policy?

- Are the various stakeholders, including women, represented in the membership and board of the organization?

- Are women from the beneficiary group represented in the structure of the organization?

- Do women from the target group have a clear influence on policy-making and implementation processes?

- Does the organization have staff with specific gender expertise and responsibilities? Where is this staff located within the organizational structure (e.g. at key/strategic points in the organization or not, with/without authority, in an advisory capacity, in a centralized unit/desk, at decentralized levels within the organization)?

- Does the organization allow space for staff who wish to organize on the basis of one aspect of their identity (e.g. sex, ethnicity, sexuality, religion, age), to inform and enrich the organization about its diversity?

- Does the organizational structure accommodate institutional learning on gender issues?

## Systems

The term 'systems' refers to processes of a diverse nature: operational/implementation, decision-making, planning, monitoring and evaluation, learning, policy-making, communication and information, sensing the environment, administration.

### Operations/implementation

- Are there procedures and mechanisms to facilitate discussions between the beneficiaries (both women and men) and the staff of the organization on gender issues?

- Are there mechanisms which enable the organization to reflect on and learn from its achievements? How do gender issues feature here (e.g. internal reflection, learning reflected in proposals and documentation, revision of original proposals)?

- Does the organization have a system for operationalizing its strategies, including targets, performance indicators, a time path and review? How is gender integrated into this system? For instance, are targets and timetables set regarding the allocation of resources towards activities aimed at women specifically, or at gender-integrated activities?

- Does the organization have a mechanism for sensing the environment in which it is working (i.e. being aware of changes in the gender force-field of actors and issues)? Is this reflected in programme proposals and activities?

- Are there mechanisms for signalling problems and conflict, for example in relation to sexual (and other forms of) harassment, and for dealing with conflict?

### Decision-making

- To what extent do beneficiaries and staff participate in decision-making in relation to management, policy-making, programme activities and external relations? Is there a difference between men and women in this respect?

- Is there a balance between control and flexibility to enable male and female staff to carry out their work? In other words, is there a balance at management level between capacity to delegate and to take decisions? How does this operate with regard to decisions concerning gender issues within the organization?

- Does the organization have a system, and does its staff have the skills, for identifying problems, analysing options and then taking the relevant decisions concerning gender issues?

*Planning, monitoring, and evaluation*
- Do methodologies for planning, monitoring, and evaluation accommodate the active participation of women beneficiaries and staff?

- Is a gender analysis, allowing for the collection of gender-disaggregated data, central to the planning (including strategic planning), monitoring and evaluation of the organization?

- Do methodologies for monitoring and evaluation accommodate listening and learning from male and female beneficiaries? And is this linked back into the planning process?

- Do the terms of references for assessment and evaluation include gender issues that address the impact on women and men, both at the level of beneficiaries and at the organizational level?

- Do planning, monitoring, evaluation, and advisory teams consist of members who are gender-sensitive and include at least one person with specific expertise and skills on gender issues?

*Communication/information*
- Does the organization's administration include records of its work in the field of gender, and are these easily accessible?

- Are staff members and the board of the opinion that the gender data of the organization and the available information on gender issues are adequate to enable them to carry out their work with gender awareness?
- Does the organization document its own learning in relation to gender practice, and does it make this information available to others?

- How is communication in the organization (e.g. between different parts of the organization) organized? Does this promote exchange, dialogue, and openness regarding gender issues?

- How is the external communication organized (e.g. with beneficiaries, with outside expertise)? Does this promote exchange, dialogue and interaction regarding gender issues?

*Personnel*
- What is the overall gender composition of staff and the board, and within the different hierarchical levels of the organization?

- Is there management commitment to the promotion of female representation at all levels of the organization (i.e. affirmative action)?

- Is this commitment set out in a policy and plan with targets and a timetable?

- Do recruitment and selection strategies facilitate the recruitment of women?

- How does the organization deal with the possible side-effects of affirmative action (e.g. disempowerment as a result of high visibility or majority group cohesion)?

- Do men and women receive equal wages for equal work?

- Does the organization promote male and female labour in non-traditional fields?

- Do the working arrangements of the organization take into account women's and men's caring responsibilities outside the workplace (e.g. part-time work, job-sharing, maternity/paternity/care leave)?

- Does the organization recognize the differences in life-time and career-time structure between women and men (also called the difference between female and male chronologies: for example, differences in terms of mobility and possibilities for working away from home for long periods)?

- Do staff (women and men) receive training on gender issues? Is this training perceived as part of an ongoing learning process of organizational change? Is it needs-based and tailor-made, addressing both attitudinal change and concrete skills?

- Does the organization appreciate both the strengths and weaknesses of its human resource base in relation to its gender policy objectives? Is this reflected in a gender-sensitive human resource plan and investment in human resources development?

- Is there clarity in the organization about people's self-interest in diversity (e.g. on the basis of sex, ethnicity, sexuality, religion, age)?

*Resources (human, financial and physical)*
- Are there adequate numbers of staff to carry out the gender programmes planned? Do staff members have the right knowledge, skills and attitude to carry out their work with gender awareness?

- Are financial resources allocated for the operationalization of the gender policy at all levels? Are these adequate?

- Are financial resources for implementation of the gender policy an integral part of the core budget?

- Are specific financial targets set for promotion of gender equality and empowerment of women among the beneficiaries?

- Are gender expertise and gender capacity building systematically budgeted for?

- Does the organization have an adequate infrastructure to enable female staff to carry out their work (e.g. in relation to a safe working environment, location of the office, transport arrangements)?

## Organizational culture

Organizational culture is what one could describe as the personality of the organization, the shared set of symbols, rituals, language, opinions and values of the organization's staff/members. This bears a direct relationship with the specific contextual and cultural setting of the organization.

- Does the organization reward or value gender-sensitive behaviour? In other words, does the organization provide incentives to enable gender-sensitive values to be implemented across the organization?

- Is there commitment throughout the organization to the implementation of the gender policy?

- Does the organization demonstrate gender-sensitive behaviour in terms of the language used, jokes and comments made, images and materials displayed, style of meetings, procedures on sexual harassment?

- Does the organization respect the diversity of styles between men and women, as a source of strength for the organization?

- Are appropriate facilities, such as lavatories, childcare, and transport, provided in the working environment?

- Do the working arrangements enable the combination of work with reproductive/caring responsibilities outside the workplace, e.g. via part-time employment, flexible working hours and leave allocations?

## External context

- Is the organization well informed about its external context, including knowledge about important actors and issues – in both positive and negative senses – with regard to gender issues?

- Is the organization building and maintaining strategic alliances with key actors in the field of gender, such as women's organizations or other organizations with gender expertise?

- Has the organization defined specific gender objectives and targets in terms of the external environment (e.g. lobbying for legislative change, influencing macro-policies, influencing public opinion, promotion of networking and cooperation between different organizations), and is it able to deal with any potential conflicts and tensions that might emerge?

## Note

1. This is an adapted version of Sarah Hlupekile Longwe's Women's Empowerment Framework, further developed by Hivos (1996) in its 'Policy Document Gender, Women and Development.' The levels should be imagined as a continuum forming a circle, with no hierarchical order or value attached.

# 10  Further bridges to cross

Recent years have seen a growing interest in understanding organizations in relation to their gender dynamics. This is not surprising. The process started at the fringes, with an occasional training or women's project. But it is now clear that good gender practice is about transforming structures, systems, and cultures: following a route which leads straight to the heart, or deep structure, of organizations and institutions, revealing their less obvious, less visible dynamics, values, norms, behaviour, and practices.

This book reflects a trend in which Northern donor agencies are becoming ready to bring the issue of gender equality back home: to practise what they preach. Reaching this point has been a process which has led them to examine the hearts and minds of their own organizations and people working in them. An increasing number of organizations and institutions, both within and outside the NGO sector, are in the process of integrating a gender perspective into their daily practice. As a consequence, the gender and development debate has moved into the field of organizational development. The book also recognizes that the debate on gender and organizational development is still at a very early stage; agencies are going through a process of learning by doing. Thus, we give a good deal of attention to frameworks, tools, and interventions that can set in motion processes of organizational change and learning as regards gender equality. We also explore key focal areas that can lead to what can be seen as a *gender quality assurance system:* for example, consistency between aspired-to and real values, openness and transparency, organizational learning, accountability, and strategic collaboration with others.

The material in the foregoing chapters is based on experiences working in our own agencies on research and case studies analysing organizations in general (in the North and the South), and on our perceptions of the gender dynamics of organizations in the South. In this closing chapter we would like to take another look at donor agencies and, specifically, their role in enabling processes of transforming gender dynamics in Southern organizations.

In any such exercise, the donor–counterpart dialogue and donor interventions need to be viewed within the global context in which NGOs – both donors and counterparts – operate. This global context is changing more rapidly than ever before, with global economic restructuring and the new communication and information technologies as its two most important features. NGOs are operating in a context in which governments, the United Nations, and international financial institutions all increasingly recognize that these organizations have a key role to play. This presents both new opportunities and new challenges. First, a rapidly changing external context requires flexibility in approaches and continuous reassessment of what might be the most adequate response. Second, the global context very often requires a global response, which points to the importance of networking and of forming strategic alliances with other actors in civil society. Third, the fact that NGOs are increasingly being taken seriously and are moving closer to centres of power in many countries raises issues of accountability and good governance, both within individual organizations and in their interrelationships. Indeed, stakeholders such as governments, other funding agencies and the general public are increasingly challenging NGOs by asking them the very questions they have raised towards others. The performance and functioning of NGOs have come into the spotlight.

Looking at these trends from the perspective of the women's movement, we can see that the processes of globalization and growing international interdependence have contributed to awareness and recognition of gender relations. The facts and figures are on the table. Today it is well known that there is no country in the world where women and men enjoy equal rights, protection, or opportunities. Important attempts have been made to change these inequalities. Global accountability mechanisms have been created, such as the Platform for Action, which was the outcome of the Fourth World Conference on Women (1995), and the UN Convention on the Elimination of All Forms of Discrimination against Women (CEDAW). States that signed these documents have committed themselves to implementing actions aimed at promoting equal rights and opportunities for women and men. Women's organizations throughout the world have played a crucial role in building these accountability mechanisms, as well as a strategic role as watchdogs and monitors of the commitments made. This has required networking, coalition building, and strategic cooperation with other actors in civil society. In many parts of the world women's organizations, through the promotion of women's human rights, also play a critical role as advocates for participatory democratic practices and the strengthening of civil society at large.

What implications do these developments have for the responsibilities of donor agencies in their roles of funding development and facilitating capacity building? Strategic alliances between change agents in donor agencies and counterpart organizations, and efforts on the part of donor agencies to facilitate gender awareness among counterpart organizations, will continue to be important. However, given the changing global context, a more diversified donor strategy is needed. What mechanisms can be set up that will enable both donor agencies and counterpart organizations to move forward in their individual and collective gender learning processes? In an external context in which, on the one hand, NGOs are coming under increasingly heavy pressure – not least from donor agencies – to perform effectively and efficiently, and, on the other hand, awareness of the unequal power relations between women and men increasingly permeates development debates and interventions everywhere, the need for checks and balances, linking and learning are high on the agenda. But this immediately raises questions: linkages with whom? accountability to whom? and how to keep the energy where it should be, that is, in enabling a process of empowerment among NGO constituencies and beneficiaries?

Enduring linkages imply the existence or development both of some kind of accountability mechanism and of a wide scope for inter-organizational learning. Further, many organizational development experts would argue that the more external linkages are made, the better. Identifying and understanding existing linkages and other accountability mechanisms is an important first step. This should result in awareness of new linkages and mechanisms that are needed, as well as suggestions about which existing ones should be strengthened. One way to build this specific form of linkage is through mutual comparisons among organizations involved in similar activities, i.e. peer comparison. This has the advantage of enabling both organizations to detect their own strengths and weaknesses and discover new opportunities and challenges. Such peer comparison also facilitates the setting of guidelines and standards for best practice. But it is also useful to compare one's own organization with organizations which are quite different, for example those in the business sector. The advantage here is that one learns new things about how organizations function, and this can stimulate creativity towards one's own organizational development strategies.

Northern donor agencies can promote inter-organizational linking and learning in the South through their funding strategies. Much is already taking place, for example in the form of workshops, exchange visits between counterparts, facilitating cooperation with local gender training institutions or consultants. Facilitating the establishment of mechanisms for peer comparison among Southern organizations, and also across regions (South–South, South–North), could be an important addition. Such an exercise can be a powerful strategy for change if the mechanism itself reflects an agreed quality assurance system. This system should be constructed by the participating organizations themselves, and should consist of key focal areas for gender equality, accompanied by indicators that reflect the specific situation and context of the organization. When the participating parties are willing to institutionalize such an exercise, inter-organizational accountability will point up the comparative advantages and disadvantages of the organizations.

Building culture- and context-specific gender quality assurance systems is a challenge. It involves answering questions such as: is it possible to develop universally applicable key focal areas? How can cultural and contextual differences be incorporated? In what ways would a gender quality assurance system be different from a general quality assurance system for organizations? Here is a whole series of further bridges to cross.

Donor agencies can also create such accountability mechanisms among themselves. *Eurostep* and Oxfam International, both networks of Northern-based secular donor agencies, have made a start by comparing gender policies and practices. In both cases the gender working groups of the networks have drafted questionnaires, which were filled in and discussed within the wider network.

Such an emphasis on lateral accountability, for donor agencies and counterparts alike, will give the concept of 'bridging the gap' a new meaning. By emphasizing the importance of consistency between internal and external policies and practices – and in that way bringing the issue back home to the donor agencies themselves – lateral accountability will facilitate a process of setting context-specific and appropriate minimum quality standards. 'Bridging the gap' could then also refer to building bridges among peer organizations, which can learn from each other through a mechanism that facilitates comparison, quality checks, and emulation. Such a process of lateral accountability could contribute to qualitative improvements in the work of NGOs, especially by becoming better equipped to respond to the opportunities and challenges presented by the global context.

Finally, as we have emphasized several times in the foregoing chapters, accountability mechanisms like openness and transparency are also highly applicable to the relationship between donor agencies and their counterpart organizations. Given the power dynamics inherent in the relationship, bridging the gap implies building in these features, in particular on the side of the donor agencies. It is therefore of critical importance to share the history of gender struggles within donor organizations, along with the ways and extent to which issues of gender inequality have been and are being addressed vis à vis counterparts. In this book, we aim, by sharing our own experiences, to express and strengthen our commitment to pursuing sustainable strategies that can promote gender equality in both our own organizations and counterpart organizations in the South.

# Appendix
# Eurostep member agencies

The following is a list of the member agencies of *Eurostep* in May 1997. Further information is available from the *Eurostep* secretariat, 115 rue Stevin, B-1040 Brussels, Belgium; tel: +32 2 231 1659/1709, fax: +32 2 230 3780; email: eurostep@gn.apc.org.

ActionAid (United Kingdom)
CNCD (Belgium)
Concern (Ireland)
Deutsche Welthungerhilfe (Germany)
Forum Syd (Sweden)
Frères des Hommes (France)
Helinas (Greece)
Hivos (Netherlands)
Ibis (Denmark)
Intermón (Spain)
KEPA (Finland)
Mani Tese (Italy)
Mellemfolkeligt Samvirke (MS) (Denmark)
Movimondo (Italy)
NCOS (Belgium)
Norwegian People's Aid (Norway)
Novib (Netherlands)
OIKOS (Portugal)
Oxfam UK/I (United Kingdom)
Swiss Coalition of Development Organizations (Switzerland)
Terre des Hommes BRD (Germany)

# Bibliography

This bibliography lists all the major references cited in the text, and also a selection of other relevant reading from recent research.

Andersen, Cecilia (1992). 'Practical guidelines', in L. Ostergaard (ed.), *Gender and development: a practical guide* (London: Routledge): 165–97.

Bacchi, Carol Lee (1996). *The politics of affirmative action: 'women', equality and category politics.* London: Sage.

Barrig, Maruja, and Andy Wehkamp (eds) (1994). *Engendering development: experiences in gender and development planning* (The Hague/Lima: Novib/Red Entre Mujeres): 73–98.

Biddulph, Steve (1995). *Manhood: an action plan for changing men's lives.* 2nd edn. Sydney: Finch Publishing.

Borren, Sylvia, Sonia Montano, Adrie Papma, and Jacque Remmerswaal (1994). *¡Somos Amigos! An evaluation of Novib's gender policy in Peru and Colombia.* No. 51 in the series of Programme Evaluations of the Co-financing Programme Novib/DGIS. The Hague: Novib/DGIS.

Brown, Helen (1994). *Women in the public and voluntary sectors: case studies in organisational change.* London: Office for Public Management.

Bruijn, de Jeanne, and Eva Cyba (eds) (1994). *Gender and organizations – changing perspectives, theoretical considerations and empirical findings.* Amsterdam: VU University Press.

Byrne, Bridget, Julie Koch Laier, with Sally Baden and Rachel Marcus (1996). *National machineries for women in development: experiences, lessons and strategies for institutionalising gender in development policy and planning.* BRIDGE Report No. 35, Institute of Development Studies, University of Sussex. Brighton: IDS.

Chigudu, Hope (1997). 'Establishing a feminist culture: the experience of Zimbabwe Women's Resource Centre and Network', *Gender and Development* 5/1 (February) (Oxfam): 35-42.

Coleman, Gillian (1991). *Investigating organisations, a feminist approach.* Occasional Paper 37, School of Advanced Urban Studies, University of Bristol. Bristol: SAUS Publications.

Collinson, David, David Knights, and Margaret Collinson (1990). *Managing to discriminate*. London: Routledge.

De Beuk (Febe Deug, Lidwi de Groot, and Dorien de Wit) (1995). *Thirty tools on diversity and organizational change*. Series of short papers prepared for 'The Art of Organizing', training sessions held in Huairou, China, during the NGO Forum of the Fourth World Conference on Women, 30 August – 8 September. Hippolytushoef, The Netherlands: De Beuk. Available from Novib in English, French, and Spanish.

Dixon, Nancy (1994). *The organizational learning cycle: How we can learn collectively*. London: McGraw-Hill.

Eade, Deborah (1991). 'How far should we push?', in Tina Wallace and Candida March (eds), *Changing perceptions: writings on gender and development* (Oxford: Oxfam), 306–10.

Everett, Jane, and Mira Savara (1994). *Women and organisations in the informal sector*. Himalaya Publishing House.
Goetz, Anne Marie (1992). 'Gender and administration', *IDS Bulletin* 23/4: 6–17.

– (1995a). 'Institutionalizing women's interests and gender-sensitive accountability in development', *IDS Bulletin* 26/3 (July): 1–10.

– (1995b). *The politics of integrating gender to state development processes: trends, opportunities and constraints in Bangladesh, Chile, Jamaica, Mali, Morocco and Uganda*. Occasional Paper for the Fourth World Conference on Women OP– 2. Geneva: UNRISD.

– (1997) 'Managing organisational change: the 'gendered' organisation of space and time', *Gender and Development* 5/1 (February) (Oxfam): 17-27.

Handy, Charles (1990). *Understanding voluntary organisations*. Harmondsworth: Penguin.

Hamerschlag, Kari, and Annemarie Reerink (1996). *Best practices for gender integration in organizations and programs from the InterAction community, findings from a survey of member agencies*. Washington: InterAction.

Hivos (1996). *Policy document gender, women and development*. The Hague.

Hofstede, Geert (1991). *Cultures and organisations, software of the mind*. London: McGraw-Hill.

Ianello, Kathleen P. (1992). *Decisions without hierarchy, feminist interventions in organization theory and practice*. London/New York: Routledge.

Itzin, Catherine, and Janet Newman (1995). *Gender, culture and organizational change: putting theory into practice.* London/New York: Routledge.

Kelleher, David, and Kate McLaren, with Ronald Bisson (1996a). *Grabbing the tiger by the tail. NGOs learning for organizational change.* Ottawa: Canadian Council for International Co-operation.

Kelleher, David, Aruna Rao, Rieky Stuart, and Kirsten Moore (1996b). 'Building a global network for gender and organizational change: work in progress'. Mimeo (Canada, 1996).

Krishnamurthy, Ranjani (1995). 'Power, institutions and gender relations: can gender training alter the equations?' Unpublished paper, available from the Gender Team, Oxfam UK/I.

Ledwith, Sue, and Fiona Colgan (1996). *Women in organisations, challenging gender politics.* London: Macmillan Press.

Longwe, Sara Hlupekile (1995). 'A development agency as a patriarchal cooking pot: the evaporation of policies for women's advancement', in Mandy Macdonald (ed.), *Women's rights and development: vision and strategy for the twenty-first century* (Oxfam Discussion Paper 6, Oxfam/One World Action): 18–29.

Macdonald, Mandy (ed.) (1994a). *Gender planning in development agencies: meeting the challenge.* Oxford: Oxfam.

– (1994b). *EUROSTEP Gender Workshop 2: Gender in partnership.* Copenhagen: MS.

– (1995). *Gender mapping the European Union.* Brussels: EUROSTEP/WIDE.

Mayoux, Linda (1994). 'Gender policy and black holes: some questions about efficiency, participation and scaling-up in NGOs.' Paper presented to Group for Development Policy and Practice, The Open University, Milton Keynes, September.

Mills, Albert J., and Peta Tancred (1992). *Gendering organizational analysis.* Newbury Park, CA/London: Sage.

Moser, Caroline (1993). 'The institutionalization of gender planning', in Caroline Moser, *Gender planning and development: theory, practice and training* (London: Routledge): 109–38.

Moss Kanter, Rosabeth (1977). *Men and women of the corporation.* New York: Basic Books.

Mukhopadhyay, Maitrayee (1995). 'Gender relations, development practice and "culture" ', *Gender and Development* 3/1 (February) (Oxfam): 15.

Nostrand, Catherine (1993). *Gender responsible leadership: detecting bias, implementing interventions.* London: Sage.

Novib (1997). 'More power, less poverty, Novib's gender and development policy until the year 2000'. The Hague: Novib.

Rao, Aruna, and David Kelleher (1995a). 'Engendering organizational change: the BRAC case', IDS *Bulletin* 26/3 (July): 69–78.

– (1995b). 'BRAC Gender Quality Action Learning Program: evaluation design'. Mimeo, 11 June.

Rao, Aruna, and Rieky Stuart (1997). 'Rethinking organisations: a feminist perspective', *Gender and Development* 5/1 (February) (Oxfam): 10–16.

Radtke, Lorraine, and Henderikus Stam, (eds) (1994). *Power/gender: social relations in theory and practice.* London: Routledge.

Schalkwyk, Johanna, Helen Thomas, and Beth Woroniuk (1996). *Mainstreaming: a strategy for achieving equality between women and men, a think piece.* Department for Policy and Legal Services, Sida. Stockholm: Sida.

Senge, Peter M, Charlotte Roberts, Richard B. Ross, Bryan J. Smith, and Art Kleiner (1994). *The fifth discipline fieldbook: strategies and tools for building a learning organization.* London: Nicholas Brealey.

Staudt, Kathleen, (ed.) (1990). *Women, international development and politics: the bureaucratic mire.* Philadephia: Temple University Press.

Swieringa, Joop, and André Wierdsma (1992). *Becoming a learning organization: beyond the learning curve.* Reading, MA: Addison Wesley.

Tannen, Deborah (1991). *You just don't understand: men and women in conversation.* London: Virago.

Tanton, Morgan (1994). *Women in management: a developing presence.* London: Routledge.